A Process of Illumination:
The Practical Guide
to Electronic Discovery

By Mary Mack, Esq.

Preface

We are pleased to present you with the third edition of "A Process of Illumination: The Practical Guide to Electronic Discovery." This updated edition includes many of the new electronic discovery issues, cases and opinions that have arisen since the first edition of this book was published in 2002. It also expands the advice provided in the practical chapters on how to prepare for e-discovery and all phases of the process – identification, preservation, collection, processing, review and production. We've included informal, narrative, "what if" scenarios of how e-discovery done right or gone wrong can affect outcome, as well as ways to protect you, your organization and/or your clients when asked to produce evidence.

With these updates, we believe we have created an informative yet highly practical guide for managing the e-discovery process. The information is applicable for both respondents to and requestors of electronically stored information (ESI). We also show how thinking proactively in a digital age – rather than reacting to each individual litigation matter – can streamline, simplify and reduce costs, risks and time involved in e-discovery.

This book is not intended to be a legal text, with every other sentence containing a citation. Other books (see the resources section) already do this very well. This is a practical guide for people who want to understand the practical aspects of e-discovery, who are looking at options to address the issues and who wish to learn some lessons from folks in the trenches. Many of the readers of the first book honored us by passing this book along to colleagues, some of whom were neither legal nor technical. We hope this edition continues to be the communication tool for bridging the gap between law, technology and business that the first edition became.

No book on the subject of e-discovery can be complete without acknowledging the contribution of the pioneers in the field: Tom Allman, Diane Barrasso, Dennis Kennedy, Bonnie Worley, Prashant Dubey, Jonathan Redgrave, Dennis Kiker, Joan Feldman, Michael Anderson, Michael Bawden, Richard Lazar, Larry Johnson, Tom Howe, Ken Withers, Florinda Baldridge, John Jesson, Tim Stevens, Jay Brudz, Mike Arkfeld, Jim Daley, Denise Howell, Michael Clark, George Socha, Michael Harnish, Fred Cabulong, Tobi Loy, Patrick Gibson, Anthony Mosquera, Belinda Runkle, Jon Eldridge, Norma Cook, Alan Winchester, Browning Marean, Tho Han, Jevon Lebar, Todd Cruz, Lyman Potts, Michael Overly, Michael Rhoden, Tom O'Connor, Chuck Kellner, Southern District Judge Shira Scheindlin, Former Magistrate Judge Ronald Hedges, Magistrate Judge Andrew Peck, Magistrate Judge David Waxse, Magistrate Judge Paul Grimm, Magistrate Judge Barbara Major, Tom Stevens, Alan Gahtan, Mark Yacano, Mike Bogdonoff, Michael Daniec, Conrad Jacoby and Bill Adams.

We also want to acknowledge and thank our team of contributing authors: Matt Deniston, Julia Wotipka, Therese Adlhoch Smith, Conrad Jacoby and Charlene Brownlee. For writing, production and editorial contributions, the Fios team acknowledges Kate Kockler, Mary Bukoski, Debbie Caldwell and Keith Lipman.

You may have specific questions not covered within the scope of this guide. Because e-discovery is undergoing rapid growth and change, new concepts and issues are constantly emerging. We always welcome your inquiries and are particularly interested in your stories – successful or otherwise. Contact us in the manner most convenient for you:

▶ E-mail us at guide@fiosinc.com

▶ Call us toll-free at (877) 700-3467 or direct at (503) 265-0700

▶ Fax us at (503) 265-0001

▶ Write to us:

Fios, Inc.
Attn: Practical Guide to e-Discovery
921 SW Washington Street, Suite 850
Portland, OR 97205

Look for updates and current articles on:
www.fiosinc.com and on discoveryresources.org

Contents

CHAPTER 1

What Happens During Electronic Discovery?

SCENARIO: A High-Level Termination.

You are thinking of firing a key employee. She's been hinting that if you do, she might file an EEOC complaint. Attempting to plan ahead for a lawsuit, you e-mail your inside and outside counsel detailing the situation, placing "attorney-client privilege"; in the subject line. "My communication should now be protected" or so you think. You do fire the key employee with all of the "Is" dotted and "T"s crossed. Six months later, she files her complaint. Her counsel sends over a document request for e-mails from the last year. Your attorneys put an immediate legal hold on e-mails and backup tapes, but the e-mails from six months ago have been overwritten as part of the organization's normal document retention policy. The IT department starts saving tapes. You are shocked to hear at trial that from the moment you sent your "privileged" e-mail to your attorneys, you had an obligation to retain material potentially relevant to the matter.[1] Your case has taken a negative turn due to this misunderstanding of what is required in the preservation phase of e-discovery and when action should have been taken.

---

1 Zubulake vs. UBS Warburg LLC, No. 02 Civ. 1243, 2003 WL 21087884 (S.D.N.Y. May 13, 2003)

LESSON LEARNED: If you are communicating, particularly in writing and especially in e-mail, with your attorneys about a situation that may evolve into legal proceedings, your attorneys need to start involving IT for preservation activities immediately. It is not enough to wait until you receive a formal notice.

This is where having established information governance principles for e-discovery, which embody legal requirements and domain expertise, is critical. Electronically stored information (ESI) must be identified, preserved and collected, using legally defensible methodologies, and moved into an evidence repository for processing and review when called upon for discovery response.

Why Zubulake is so Important

The case of Zubulake v UBS Warburg flushed out a wide range of e-discovery and spoliation issues and is considered by many to be the philosophical underpinnings of the 2006 amendments to the Federal Rules of Civil Procedure (FRCP). United States District Court Judge Shira A. Scheindlin issued five ground-breaking opinions in this case, helping to establish a baseline for e-discovery practices in modern litigation. These included:

- *The scope of a party's duty to preserve electronic evidence during the course of litigation*

- *A counsel's duty to monitor their clients' compliance with electronic data preservation and production*

- *Data sampling recommendations and guidelines*

- *The ability for the disclosing party to shift the costs of restoring "inaccessible" back up tapes to the requesting party*

- *The imposition of sanctions for the spoliation (or destruction) of electronic evidence*

Interestingly, while spoliation judgments were relatively rare in the era of paper discovery, they are more common for ESI. The sanctions can be severe. Besides legal costs and fines, the ultimate penalty – the summary judgment – lurks for corporations that have not shown good faith in their information governance and legal hold policies or that appear to 'drag their feet' when an e-discovery request is made. According to records management policy expert Laura Kibbe, Esq., former e-discovery counsel at Pfizer, "Don't play 'hide the ball' with the opposition when it comes to e-evidence. Negotiate scope and need early on."

Defining Electronic Discovery

Electronic discovery is: the identification, preservation, collection, processing, review and distribution of ESI associated with legal and government proceedings.

ESI, as defined in most requests for production, includes all types of electronically created evidence, such as e-mail messages and associated file attachments (the e-mail "chain"), memos, reports, plain text files, spreadsheets, digital art and photos, presentations, data stored in proprietary databases, voice mails, instant messages, and any other data that is created or stored on a computer, computer network or other electronic storage media. The 2006 amendments to the FRCP specifies ESI as "including writings, drawings, graphs, charts, photographs, sound recordings, images, and other data or data compilations — stored in any medium from which information can be obtained either directly or, if necessary, after translation by the responding party into a reasonably usable form."[2]

That's the dry description.

In reality, e-discovery presents a paradigm shift from the single dimension of traditional document discovery into the new age of digital information. Unlike paper evidence, electronic evidence is multi-dimensional, potentially "virtual" as it's not necessarily tied to or under the control of a single user, and rarely can be destroyed without leaving tell-tale signs. These signs may themselves become responsive in a matter. ESI for e-discovery can reside anywhere – on laptops, office PCs, network servers, enterprise content and records management systems, USB thumb drives, Personal Digital Assistants (PDAs), CD-ROMs, DVD-ROMs, MP3 players, Blackberries, smart cell phones, backup tapes, flash memory cards, other archive media and third-party storage systems.

Over the past few years, there has been an explosion of different file types due to new technology on the market. One handy Internet reference site for educating yourself about the various file types that could be encountered during the course of a typical production is: http://filext.com/. Currently, the site claims over 24,000 reported file extensions and growing. It is important to remember that many

---

2 FRCP 34(a)(1)(A)

of the file extensions that could be contained on a typical laptop may be an executable file or system file that might not have any bearing on the case. The amendments to the FRCP require early discussions between counsel and internal IT departments, so that ESI requirements, and the systems in which potentially relevant evidence is stored, are fully understood. The amended rules also seek to reduce the number of disputes that necessitate judicial intervention by requiring parties to negotiate their positions early in the process, as adjusting collection, production and review procedures can become increasingly difficult as time passes.

As technology advances, litigation support systems are becoming more sophisticated in order to accommodate the new ESI types that are being used in the ordinary course of business. For example, with unified messaging, also known as Voice over IP, being used instead of a traditional telephone, voice mails and audio recordings are becoming more accessible as digital evidence and collectable as e-mail. This new digital content generates metadata as it is forwarded, downloaded, archived, copied or moved and can also become part of litigation. Once considered too costly to review or access, new collection and review tools are redefining how audio evidence is treated during discovery.

It is this broad potential scope of the ESI universe that can intimidate those new to the concept. Unlike paper evidence, ESI is far more voluminous, easily replicated and distributed than hard copy. It includes unseen metadata, chains and threads that can be more significant than the original content itself.

Recent cases have highlighted the serious consequences of mishandling ESI in civil litigation. The Coleman vs. Morgan Stanley decision,[3] in which ESI issues led to a record $1.45 billion jury verdict, is only one of the high-visibility cases where ESI mismanagement caused great damage to a litigant's case. The amended rules have addressed this demonstrable lack of understanding on the part of outside counsel as to their client's IT systems and its relevance to specific litigation matters. The rules have been amended, in part, to avoid the Morgan Stanley-like situations, where the case was decided without fully reaching its merits. The FRCP now require

---

3 Coleman (Parent) Holdings, Inc. v. Morgan Stanley & Co. Inc., No. CA, 15th Jud. Cir., Palm Beach Cty., Fla., Mar. 23, 2005

technical assistance in preparing initial disclosures and in responding to interrogatories and requests for production. ESI needs to be discussed as part of party disclosures or responses made pursuant to amended FRCP Rules 26, 33 and 34.

Because of the differences between traditional discovery and e-discovery, spoliation is a bigger issue than it ever was with conventional documents. Without clear records retention policies and defensible evidence preservation and collection policies, spoliation risks abound. Pleading ignorance will not win you any points with the judge, as was demonstrated in Morgan Stanley.

ESI, and failure to manage it properly, is the source of much unnecessary cost and risk. "More money is probably spent litigating e-discovery problems than in litigating class actions," said Ken Withers when he was the senior education attorney at the Washington-based Federal Judicial Center, the research arm of the U.S. courts. "This is part of potentially every case in the 21st Century." Ken is now at the influential Sedona Conference, which is a group that formed out of the need to focus the dialogue on forward-looking principles, best practices and guidelines in specific areas of the law that may have a dearth of guidance or are otherwise at a "tipping point."[4]

The Sedona Conference published "The Sedona Principles Addressing Electronic Document Production," Second Edition (June, 2007),[5] which walks the public through 14 basic principles of e-discovery that should be used in combination with federal and state rules in order to help lawyers navigate their way through complex litigation that requires production of ESI. It provides additional guidelines regarding preservation obligations, initial disclosures and production specifics. (see Appendix A)

Talk is Cheap…And is Now Required

The FRCP, Sedona Principles and the Electronic Discovery Reference Model (EDRM)[6] are changing conversations between opposing counsel, and between counsel and IT. Historically,

---

4 http://www.thesedonaconference.org/content/tsc_mission/show_page_html

5 http://www.thesedonaconference.org/dltForm?did=TSC_PRINCP_2nd_ed_607.pdf

6 www.edrm.net

corporations and outside counsel have resisted discovery requests on grounds that the material sought by a requesting party is not responsive, irrelevant or unduly burdensome with limited benefit to the requesting party. Discovery of ESI has been a major battleground for undue burden arguments, with mixed results. Different judges, even in the same jurisdiction, have looked at similar fact patterns and have reached seemingly contradictory conclusions about the true effort required to collect and produce certain types of ESI. One court even concluded that RAM, the memory in your computer that refreshes every time you boot, is ESI.[7] Imagine the forensics bills to preserve RAM.

In public comments regarding the initial revisions to the FRCP, members of the Civil Rules Advisory Committee repeatedly stated that they were frustrated by counsels' inability to discuss e-discovery issues, much less agree on any logistical details, absent affirmative intervention by the courts. One intentional result of the amended language in FRCP rules 16 and 26 is to force counsel to raise the topic of ESI and its potential relevance in "meet and confer" sessions in advance of a scheduling conference with the court. Discussing ESI does not mean that it will always be relevant to a dispute. It remains possible that some disputes may involve little if any ESI. However, to the extent that counsel can agree on ESI, the repositories in which it is stored, and what is in and out of scope, parties will have a much clearer, common understanding as to their respective preservation and production obligations.

The diagram below illustrates how the FRCP amendments have impacted the e-discovery process. For additional guidance, you can also consult the "Civil Discovery Standards" published by the American Bar Association and the Conference of Chief Justices' "Guidelines for State Trial Courts."

Rule	Description	Intent	Reality
Rule 16 (b)	Allows the court to establish rules around disclosure, privilege, methods and work product prior to electronic discovery commencing	Save court and attorney time by pre-establishing rules & process for managing discovery	Legal must understand IT environment for all federal cases within first 120 days, more motion practice around ED very early in case; court order higher stakes than party agreement

---

7 Columbia Pictures Indus. v. Bunnell, 2007 WL 2080419 (C.D. Cal. May 29, 2007)

Rule 26 (a)	Adds "electronically stored information" (ESI) as own category	Remove ambiguity around the words "document" and "data compilations"	No more wriggle room for instant messaging, Voice over IP, databases, PDA's
Rule 26 (b)(2)	Sets up two-tier discovery for accessible and inaccessible data; provides procedures for cost shifting on inaccessible data	Remove uncertainty about who pays for requests for restoring backup tapes, forensics; make sure Zubulake remains a one-circuit precedent	Will require more work and costs for defendants very early in a case to account for the backups and what data is on them; codifies Zubulake for entire US
Rule 26 (b)(5)	Clarifies procedures when privileged ESI is inadvertently sent over to the requesting party (retrieval of that information)	To allow "clawback" of privileged information; allow parties to push the cost of review to the requestor	Still huge risks involved; will not be able to capture/ retrieve all sensitive data (e.g. trade secrets and other IP), embarrassing e-mails, waiver of privilege for other cases
Rule 26 (f)	Requires all parties to sit down together before discovery begins to agree on some form of protocol	Rule encourages uniformity, structure and more predictable motion practice	Opportunity to shift preservation costs if prepared for these discussions; otherwise opportunity to get painted into a corner
Rule 33 (d)	Includes ESI as part of the business records related to interrogatories	To reduce time spent gathering and analyzing data to answer interrogatories	Can provide transaction detail in electronic form in answer to interrogatories; may need to provide direct access or decent tools
Rule 34 (b)	Establishes protocols for how documents are produced to requesting parties	Stop arguments about the form of production, decide early to save costs	Requesting party gets to choose form of production; most advantageous form is native files which are more difficult to review and have potentially damaging metadata or track changes
Rule 37 (e)	Provides "safe harbor" when electronic evidence is lost and unrecoverable as a matter of regular business processes	Help calm fears (and avoid sanctions) when data is lost or overwritten in the normal course of business (gut Zubulake)	Puts GC on notice to ensure litigation holds and data destruction policies are legally defensible; hard to prove without third-party validation (codifies Zubulake)
Rule 37 (f)	Allows for sanctions against parties unwilling to participate in the 26(f) discovery conference planning process	Bring collaboration and agreement to the discovery process in the early stages of litigation	Places a greater requirement on both parties to be prepared for the "meet and confer" negotiations
Rule 45	Subpoenas to produce documents includes ESI	Clarifies rules for subpoenas to ensure consistency	No more arguing whether ESI is a "document"
Form 35	Standardizes discovery agreements	Avoid downstream delays and motion practice around discovery	Automatic reminder to include ESI where it is often overlooked

Organizational Litigation Readiness

FCRP Rule 26(f) requires parties to discuss e-discovery issues prior to the scheduling conference. Some, but not all, state courts have also established additional protocols that have further defined the expectations of the "meet and confer." The United States District Court for the District of Maryland has issued an ESI Protocol[8], which mandates dialogue between counsel regarding the specifics of IT architecture and production specifics. As part of the "meet and confer," counsel must be prepared to discuss the details of an organization's internal network. Some provisions of the prescriptive Maryland protocol include determining where ESI subject to the litigation is maintained, including:

> a) Format, location, structure, and accessibility of active storage, back-up and archives
>
> b) Servers
>
> c) Computer systems, including legacy systems
>
> d) Remote and third party locations
>
> e) Back-up Media (for disaster) vs. back-up media for archival purposes/record retention laws
>
> f) Network, intranet and shared areas (public folders, discussion databases, departmental drives, and shared network folders)
>
> g) Desktop computers and workstations
>
> h) Portable media, laptops, personal computers, PDAs, paging devices, mobile telephones and flash drives
>
> i) Tapes, discs, drives, cartridges and other storage media
>
> j) Home computers (to the extent, if any, they are for business purpose)
>
> k) Paper documents that represent ESI

---

8 http://www.mdd.uscourts.gov/news/news/ESIProtocol.pdf

This listing of ESI is the simplest part of the Maryland protocol. It also includes specific directions to exchange information about systems BEFORE the meet and confer, sets out a framework to discuss preservation, and defines the form of production (including with or without metadata).

In order to be prepared for the meet and confer process, you need to start by assessing your organization's or client's readiness to adequately represent and produce ESI. Are you able to identify sources of relevant data from the above list? Are there consistent and enforced preservation protocols in place? What technologies and processes are being utilized for the collection, review and production of the ESI? Imagine that you have a "business-ending" lawsuit or investigation and need to produce ESI within 30 days. Who would be on the team? Who understands the IT systems? What segments of the business are most impacted? What guidance is needed from outside counsel or third-party experts? Do you have a central, accountable expert that can translate technical concepts into everyday English and who can work together with counsel, IT, compliance, records management, litigation support, case managers, e-discovery providers and expert witnesses?

Some who have not implemented litigation readiness plans have suffered severe consequences. Magistrate Judge Barbara Major sanctioned the outside counsel for Qualcomm by mandating they work with Qualcomm to get to root cause after an e-discovery debacle and to create a litigation response plan.[9] Litigation readiness is no longer just for corporations.

What's Important for Individuals in Various Roles to Consider?

The hazards and opportunities of ESI vary depending on your role or position on the discovery response team and which side of the litigation you're on. Here are some examples of how the new realities of e-discovery can impact you:

---

9 QUALCOMM INCORPORATED, Plaintiff v. BROADCOM CORPORATION, Defendant and Related Counterclaims. No. 05cv1958-B (BLM).

Executive Management

SCENARIO: Shredding electronic data

The Attorney General has been engaging you in conversations about practices at your organization. No papers have been received by your firm yet. Your executive team is getting nervous. News reporters are calling to run down rumors in the business press. You've heard hallway discussions about "Evidence Eliminator," a "wiping" program that is the electronic equivalent of the paper shredder. It is supposed to really delete files, not the kind of deletions the hapless Arthur Andersen people accomplished.[10] Should you intervene to stop employees from wiping their drives, or would it be better to look the other way?

SHREDDING ELECTRONIC DATA

LESSON LEARNED: Just as with conventional documents and discovery, signs of intentional destruction or attempts at hiding evidence will not reflect favorably on your case. Document

---

10 Although the Arthur Andersen decision was ultimately reversed, it was done so on the grounds of improper and overly broad instructions to the jury, not on the issue of electronic evidence retention policies and spoliation. In the meantime, the whole debacle of Enron and Arthur Andersen's inconsistently applied policy of records retention ended up destroying the company. Congress has also enacted laws since Andersen that require document retention in situations like those illustrated in the case. In 2002, Congress enacted the Sarbanes-Oxley Act, partially in response to Andersen. Among other things, the Act imposes various retention requirements on publicly traded companies and imposes liability on their chief executive and financial officers for violation of such requirements.

retention and destruction policies must be implemented under neutral conditions and consistently followed to demonstrate good faith and to avoid hints of obstruction. Randomly picking and choosing what to retain and what to destroy is not a records retention policy. Be aware that the programs you use can become evidence in and of themselves.

In one case contested in federal court in Chicago, a company was punished after its owner bought a copy of a software program, called Evidence Eliminator, to erase files from his computer. The judge in the case threatened that the owner's suit against a rival over patent infringement be thrown out because of the owner's "egregious conduct." The judge forced the offender to pay a portion of his opponent's fees and costs.[11]

Do you really want to have your witnesses explain how or why they used Evidence Eliminator?

Even with wiping programs, forensics can look into nooks and crannies that wiping programs can miss. There will be evidence that the wiping program was installed, which will put your firm or company in a bad light, unless your document retention policies specify wiping and it is done on a regular basis, well before your conversations with the Attorney General. Of course, even then, you need to stop wiping when you believe a lawsuit is possible, and most certainly if you receive a preservation order or a spoliation letter. It's important to make it clear that no one is helping by deleting files. Send out the litigation hold notices in multiple formats, including e-mail, letter, voice mail and in-person meetings. Make sure the wording is strong enough to mandate preservation activities. Monitor and document compliance towards creating a record of "good faith." Continually re-issue the order until the legal hold has been satisfied. Remember that the record may become public. Be careful about intertwining strategy with directives to preserve and other supporting documentation.

---

11 "Costly e-discovery `part of potentially every case in the 21st Century," Chicago Tribune Online Edition, April 10, 2005.

Inside Counsel

SCENARIO: Your company has made headline news (for the wrong reasons)

A workplace tragedy has occurred, and your friends and executive management are in the hot seat. The government is inquiring, and your shareholders are suing. This could be a company-ending event. Suddenly, from all sides, you are being asked to manage and respond to six different law firms, each handling a different aspect of this same matter. Your insurance company is paying to defend the company, and the counsel they have chosen needs access to the organization's most sensitive data. How do you give them access to only the material they request in a secure environment outside of your firewalls?

The lawyers from all those different firms are monopolizing the people in IT who are responsible for keeping the business running. IT is complaining that some lawyers want last year's e-mail, some want this year's e-mail, and some want to send in a black bag collection team to forensically sweep the entire executive suite.

LESSON LEARNED: Collect once, produce often! When you are involved in multiple litigations, it's important to identify key people involved in each one. Issue coding will change across cases, impacting the responsiveness of an item. You can gain a time advantage by reviewing material for both junk and privilege only once while adding a verification step for different counsel. This saves money and reduces risk of producing privileged items in different litigation and serves as a junk filter across multiple litigations. By planning ahead, having repeatable processes in place and reducing duplicative reviews, you can lower the costs of the collective litigations, create more favorable outcomes, minimize the impact of litigation on the people running your company, and benefit the company's bottom line.[12]

SCENARIO: Getting ready for common matters

Perhaps you are not faced with a crisis, as in the previous scenario.

---

12 "Litigation Readiness: An Executive Primer," by Prashant Dubey. 2008. Contact Fios for more information.

In fact, your days may be quiet, with nothing more shattering than an occasional employee departing, but with company assets, or a disgruntled ex-employee threatening a suit. Is there a low cost way to protect the company from these common threats without going overboard? Remember, $27 million later, Zubulake was still a one-plaintiff employment claim.

LESSON LEARNED: First, make it policy to collect or preserve in place all potentially relevant ESI stored on the hard drives and servers used from all departing employees' machines, with documentation to prove chain of custody. If the computers are not actively needed, the cost-effective option is to remove the hard drives completely and replace them with new drives before re-deploying the equipment, unless you have deployed forensic software with a trained staff. Store collected ESI in a secure repository, perhaps offsite with a third party. If the departing employee sues, the chances are good that there is something in the preserved data set that you can use for impeachment. Without the preserved ESI, the ex-employee can testify that you destroyed evidence favorable to them, meeting one of the Zubulake factors.

Relatively simple safeguards go a long way. Should a matter arise, obtaining ESI from the employee's own preserved machine is comparatively easy and low cost. Many companies derive business value by isolating employee work product and distributing it to the other employees who need it. The drives need not be kept forever.

With records management in place, you can develop a procedure to take the ESI from ex-employees, hard drives, classify it and retain or dispose of it in accordance with the organization's records retention and legal hold policies.

There are other steps that can be taken, which are covered later in this book.

GET SERIOUS WITH IT

SCENARIO: Get serious with IT

Imagine that you and the CIO have never gotten along, and you feel she's never really understood the legal ramifications of the company's IT policies nor paid attention to your requests. Recently, you sent her a preservation letter for a matter. Now you and her top e-mail administrator are sitting at the deposition table. The e-mail administrator is answering the question, "What is your e-mail retention policy?" She gives the business-as-usual answer of "30 days." You trust that he will surely go on to explain that he received a preservation letter causing him to suspend that policy for this matter. He is asked, "Is that policy still in place today?" Your heart begins pounding in your ears as you take in the implication of his answer: "Yes." You call for a recess. Sure, the CIO forwarded the preservation letter to the e-mail administrator; however, you vaguely recall hearing about an upgrade to the e-mail system and IT being shorthanded. Obviously, the importance of your request was not understood by the e-mail administrator nor did the CIO follow up to enforce it.

LESSON LEARNED: Get written verification that your orders to IT are being taken seriously. Ask about the "who's" and "how's" of getting preservation done. You may be able to assist IT in getting supplemental funds for the new tapes and resources needed to comply. Have frequent, informal conversations and engender an atmosphere of trust and partnership.

Increasingly, the courts are holding counsel more responsible for assuring that preservation duties and destruction holds are enforced. For example, the Zubulake case discusses counsel's preservation obligation. "Counsel must oversee compliance with the litigation hold, monitoring the party's efforts to retain and produce the relevant documents....[I]t is not sufficient to notify all employees of a litigation hold and expect that the party will then retain and produce all relevant information."[13] Judge Scheindlin put the obligation on inside and outside counsel to monitor the preservation effort.

SCENARIO: Know what's possible and keep tabs on outside counsel

Your company is in a class action law suit. Your outside counsel sends "form responses" back to the plaintiffs denying any electronic documents existed (read: they don't understand e-discovery). Not amused, the judge orders your company to produce and, just for good measure, to not delete any data from "anywhere." Your CIO tells you there are batch processes that empty out transaction files, meaning that programming will be necessary to keep the files intact per the order.

Meanwhile, e-mails are piling up, and IT is afraid to load balance the servers because they do not want to run afoul of the judge's preservation order. Your outside counsel says they will help you get the order overturned, but it will take 4 months, which is more time than your business has to make sure the infrastructure does not keel over.

You've always wanted a seat at the executive table. You may now get the chance because you can safeguard the company from such risks in the future. You are beginning to understand both law and technology and will be sure to reach out for help as needed, as well as monitor your outside counsel for their e-discovery savvy from now on.

LESSON LEARNED: Especially in the early part of a large class action or product liability case, monitor the responses of your outside counsel, so you do not end up backed into a corner. Plan for a long siege. Partner with your IT counterparts as you will need favors from them. Their actions can make or break your

---

13 Zubulake V, 2004 WL 1620866 (S.D.N.Y, July 20, 2004)

credibility in a case. Because large cases, such as class actions, have a local component, you will need someone internal or from a third party who can facilitate communication deep into a corporate IT structure.

Boilerplate objections are becoming an artifact as the 2006 amendments to the FRCP reshape the e-discovery landscape. Form responses, combined with a motion to compel from your opponent, could equal serious sanctions or worse.

Outside Counsel

Even if you consider yourself well-informed about e-discovery, you'll want to reduce your malpractice exposure by keeping an eye on e-discovery partners and service providers and by staying in charge of the high-level decisions. Especially early in the evolution of e-discovery, many organizations tasked their internal IT departments to process evidence internally. Many times, these organizations did not understand the legal functional requirements before they began. As a result, metadata changed, and ESI was missed by inspection and search. A gap in communication between outside counsel and IT was very common, creating a threat to both counsel and client. The pendulum swung to outsourcing all e-discovery to outside counsel and is now swinging back to insourcing inside the corporation.

Consider the Morgan Stanley case:

Headline: "Morgan Stanley to Fire Law Firm," Morgan Stanley, vilified by a state court judge for failing to produce documents in a high-profile legal fight with financier Ronald Perelman, is moving to replace its main law firm in the case...The Wall Street brokerage house said it has become clear that the court "has lost all confidence in any statement or representation made" by lawyers at Kirkland and Ellis LLP., and that Morgan Stanley has put the firm...on notice 'of a potential malpractice claim' arising out if its representation."[14]

---

14 Wall Street Journal – March 23, 2005

SCENARIO: Cross-organizational team is not clicking

At trial, a key witness discloses documents that should have been turned over after the lead partner repeatedly certified that discovery was complete. A young associate could not communicate the documents' relevance to senior partners even though they were called out in a deposition and at trial. A subsequent keyword search found hundreds of thousands of pages, also not produced. As the magistrate judge considers sanctions, your request to abrogate the privilege is partially granted for work product, but not on the all-important communications. Adding insult to injury, after being replaced by the client, you faced potential sanctions, including referral to the disciplinary bar and the potential requirement to notify each client and tribunal of your e-discovery misbehavior.

LESSON LEARNED: Trust, accountability and process can allow everyone to sleep at night. Having someone to manage e-discovery red alerts (i.e. receiving non-produced documents at a deposition), respond to the judge's repeated requests for certifications or assurances, and monitor the reduction and review protocols will allow the case to be tried on the merits, not on e-discovery tactics. While in this scenario the sanctions were ultimately lifted and sent back to the magistrate for a "re-do," the trust between outside and inside counsel was broken (see Qualcomm v. Broadcom).[15]

KNOW WHAT'S POSSIBLE. KEEP TABS ON VENDORS.

---

15 Qualcomm Inc. v. Broadcom Corp., No. 05-CV-1958-B (BLM), United States District Court for the Southern District of California

SCENARIO: Choose higher level partners

Your e-discovery services provider has just informed you that they cannot get data off key backup tapes. You trust them and bring that information to court. The court orders the tapes to be given to the opposition. To your embarrassment, the opposition's expert restores them in a few days and finds responsive data.[16]

LESSON LEARNED: Verify claims of impossibility with other vendors. Be careful to allow enough time to obtain second opinions. Waiting until a week before the discovery cut-off date will put your back to the wall. Choose a reliable e-discovery partner who has a proven track record of success, sophistication and history of dealing with diverse challenges and data types – one that will provide credibility via affidavit or testimony.

SCENARIO: Don't automatically assume your firm should host the data

You are representing a client in a class action. Another law firm representing the client in a different jurisdiction needs access to the ESI involved in your client's case. You are currently reviewing the evidence on your firm's system. Your litigation support department has just told you it will take at least two months to procure and install the equipment and processes necessary to allow another firm access to your firm's network.

LESSON LEARNED: Consider who will need to access the ESI before choosing where to host it. Consider using third parties, such as e-discovery experts and providers, to minimize the impact on your firm's systems and daily business, and to maintain the ability to respond quickly to review requests. Issues of client confidentiality, office security, chain of custody, preservation of metadata and accessibility can make your own law firm the least favorable place to host the data.[17] Because possession (of the data) is nine-tenths of the law, when outside counsel collaborate it is important to consider the dynamics. Law firms have varying degrees of sophistication in e-discovery and ability to collaborate in an adversarial environment. Infighting and blaming can impact

16 Residential Funding Corp. v. DeGeorge Financial Corp. 306 F. 3d 99 (2nd Cir. 2002)

17 "Essentials of e-Discovery: Finding and Using Cyber Evidence," by Joan E. Feldman, Glasser LegalWorks, 2003.

the cohesiveness of a defense team unless the client places a high value on collaboration.

If the enterprise collects, processes and hosts its own data, it is critical that outside counsel understand, and can stand behind, the processes and procedures used to collect, reduce and produce the evidence. Not all cases should be hosted internally, even in the most experienced law firms or enterprises. Backdating, subprime and other cases where fraud may be alleged would indicate that a third party shield should be considered.

CIOs and IT Directors

SCENARIO: Meet and Confer

You've read the papers about a new federal case involving a defective product. You make a mental note to self on the way into the office, "In about 2 years from today, I can expect a panic call from the attorneys for a 'quick-turn collect and produce' from about 50 people." You get your coffee and are surprised when your inside counsel, accompanied by three other people, are sitting in your office. It turns out the rules have changed. Not only do you have to help with the preservation targeting, you're being asked for a schedule of what you can collect, by when and, further, what's on all those backup tapes. And, by the way, this is how it will be for all federal and many state cases of a certain exposure, not just those that escape settlement or motions to dismiss.

LESSON LEARNED: It is time to get in the loop with legal. CIOs and IT directors used to be the last to know that they hold responsibility and accountability for producing evidence-quality ESI to meet the demands of outside counsel and the courts. Many corporations segregate discussions on sensitive legal matters to those who "need to know." Counsel used to procrastinate in determining an e-discovery approach, hoping a case would settle or that they could negotiate a "gentleman's agreement" not to request electronic data.

Now, the issues regarding ESI will largely be addressed in the first 120 days of a lawsuit being served.

It is imperative to know who among your team you can trust to deliver quickly and to work well with the special communication challenges with attorneys. Your new friends in legal may be able to help you with a special allocation for your unfunded mandate.

SCENARIO: New technology purchase

After a year of negotiations, you will finally get your Voice over IP (VoIP) system, which will save the organization hundreds of thousands of dollars in long distance charges. You suddenly receive a call from the CEO. Legal has put the cabosh on the system until they can put in place preservation, collection, review and production procedures for those employees under legal hold. What happened?!!

LESSON LEARNED: Have someone at the table who can articulate and document legal functional business requirements before going out to bid. Avoid last-minute scuttling by involving legal in the process from the beginning. See the chapter on technology counsel, and consider partnering with legal to sponsor a person or chartering a team. Incorporating legal's requirements will save the company money and reduce legal risk exposure.

Technologies developed for normal business purposes often lack compliance features necessary in today's e-discovery climate, such as the ability to place a selective hold on ESI or to export data without changing dates.

SCENARIO: Mergers and acquisitions

Your company is about to merge with another. You are notified that your attorneys need to review five years of evidence for eight departments at three locations involving 80 people (custodians). The ESI needs to be at the attorney's office next week. There is no court deadline, but the deal needs to close in the next 45 days or the terms change. A delay will subtract $20 million from the bottom line, as the price is tied to stock prices at a particular point in time. You look at your staff allocation and see that the key IT personnel are out on vacation, and their designees are consumed with fighting fires to keep normal business operations running.

LESSON LEARNED: Train your emergency response team in the proper way to collect evidence, and have a third-party partner on deck who can be trusted to meet your needs before a situation like this occurs.

UNHAPPY DEPARTURE OF A COMPANY PRESIDENT.

SCENARIO: Unhappy departure of a company president

Attorneys for an ousted president are asking for electronic data from his old computer. However, because IT budgets were so tight, all spare computers were routinely re-deployed. The computer belonging to the departed president was returned "broken" and sent back to the manufacturer for new hardware and an operating system upgrade. ESI was overwritten in the process, and, for the data that did survive, it was difficult to prove chain of custody. Despite all this, a forensic expert was able to recover lurid third-party e-mails and deleted commission files. This evidence allowed a favorable settlement for the company.

LESSON LEARNED: Don't be penny-wise and pound-foolish when it comes to IT policies, such as reuse of computers, without preserving hard drives. This can complicate e-discovery further down the road. If you do need to recover ESI, rely on experts to obtain it correctly and maintain its integrity and credibility. Also, train your employees that short of running the computer over with a car, deleted data can come back to haunt them.

Litigation Support

Many times, the electronic buck stops with the staff responsible for litigation support. This can be risky, especially if your attorneys are unfamiliar with the differences between hard copy and digital review, or if they don't fully comprehend the pitfalls of gathering electronic data yourself.

LUDITE IN A HURRY.

SCENARIO: Luddite in a hurry

Your attorneys have a case that involves a lot of electronic evidence. But they are so computer phobic, they don't even answer their own e-mail. They have no idea what they're in for. A partner naively asks you to print out the 50 CDs worth of ESI, which have been gathering dust on his desk for the last two weeks, so he can review it "over the weekend at home." He doesn't realize you will need a moving van to ship the boxes of paper he's asked to review. Now, you are frantically calling print vendors to assist you on the Friday before Memorial Day, hoping to have something for him to review on Saturday.

LESSON LEARNED: Know your limitations (and theirs), and get expert help. ESI is different from paper documentation and is more voluminous than some attorneys imagine. Plan ahead, and make sure your attorneys are well educated. Have relationships built with outside providers to handle your overflow, peak periods and emergencies.

SCENARIO: In-house review

Your firm expects you to go out and collect the client's ESI. You have a modicum of computer knowledge (probably more than the attorneys do), so you confidently go to the site and begin interviewing witnesses. The witnesses point out key documents, which you burn to CDs. You bring the CDs back to the law firm and dump them on a big server. But it's not that easy. After cleaning up the virus attack you've picked up from the client's files, and apologizing to the firm's other clients for the spam war it launched, your firm's IT department finally gives you offline resources to perform review.

LESSON LEARNED: Don't assume you know how to collect electronic evidence correctly for legal purposes. Be careful about reviewing client data on your own machines. Take precautions, such as working off of copies, virus scanning and using machines isolated from your network.

SCENARIO: Selective review at the client site

You click around and open a few documents at the desktop of each witness to make sure they are responsive and not privileged. You then burn a CD to bring back to the office. You copy the many CDs to your law firm server and use standard Windows® search tools to determine relevance and potential privilege. You print the documents for the attorneys to review.

At trial, a key piece of evidence is now in question because the "Create Date" comes later than the "Modified Date." Why? Because you didn't understand how to extract and protect a native file – you merely copied files from one device to another, which altered the metadata and authenticity. Your firm is now being sued for malpractice because it appears that an agent of the firm, you, has altered key evidence.

Inside the file, when it is looked at forensically, your name appears. That's how they know you are involved.

Only later on, during your experience on the stand, do you learn that CDs have a different operating system, over-stamping key dates with the date of collection. You learn that opening up Microsoft Office documents on your computer can cause your name to be embedded in the document, particularly if you print it out. "Autosave" features can get you in trouble too by muddling metadata.

LESSON LEARNED: Produce ESI from a source that has not been altered. Have a third-party expert collect relevant ESI using collection procedures appropriate to the level the evidence demands. Preserve native files, so it is possible to produce from the unaltered file and protect the admissibility of the evidence. Rarely can in-house litigation support staff manage all aspects of ESI collection correctly or quickly. Communicate to the partners, where appropriate, how their requests are different when ESI is involved.

SCENARIO: Produce native files

You are on a team required to produce native files. A key spreadsheet has social security numbers on it and calculations you'd rather not have exposed to the opposition. You erase the personally identifiable information (ssn's). Then you discover a cool feature that will allow the results of the calculations to be frozen and the underlying formulas erased. A blistering decision later, you are forced to produce the spreadsheet, formulas intact.[18]

LESSON LEARNED: Native file production needs special consideration as overzealous scrubbing can make it look like you are hiding something.

Hopefully these war stories entertained and you and provided some useful background and lessons from the real world.

But remember, despite the potential complexities of individual cases and scenarios, the key steps of e-discovery remain the same, regardless of the specifics of the litigation or investigation:

1. Strategy
2. Preservation
3. Collection
4. Processing
5. Review
6. Production

These steps provide the framework for the process you need to follow in order to reduce risk and maximize benefits from e-discovery. During each step, there are specific activities that can further solidify your position, if followed properly. Some are simply good practice, such as researching the opposition, anticipating requests and developing a defense. Others are mandatory and specific to electronic data, such as collecting and preparing ESI.

---

18 Williams v. Sprint/United Mgmt. Co., 2006 WL 1867478 (D. Kan. July 1, 2006)

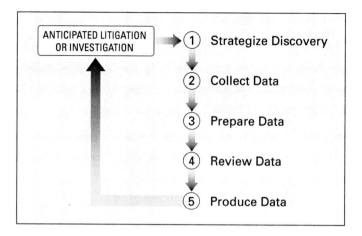

Successful e-discovery starts with strategy development and negotiation with the opposition. Done early on, this sets the scope of discovery and establishes the preservation responsibility. From there, you can proceed through a methodical progression of data collection, processing, review and production.

You've received a production of electronic files

SCENARIO: You've received a terabyte (TB) of native files as a result of a judge granting your motion to compel production in a form that can be digested by your firm. What a victory to convince the judge that those three dumb terminals, available 9-to-5 for a page-by-page review, would require many thousands of days of review. Your attorneys slapped a searching tool on the server and started searching away, opening documents and e-mailing them back and forth amongst themselves. They've found electronic documents directly contradicting depositions. Your attorneys now want to introduce these documents into evidence, but the "modify" date on the file is after the date they were produced to you.

LESSON LEARNED: When receiving native files, treat it as a forensic event. Image the media and keep an evidentiary copy. You may get lucky. and the producing party may reuse media and your forensics could surface other items. Of course, if it surfaces privileged items, you may need to give them back under ethical rules or a "clawback" agreement, but this isn't criminal law where all the "fruits of the poison tree" are excluded from evidence. Once your evidence copy is made, search and review any way you want, but when it comes time for production, produce from the evidence copy. Make sure you have a hash of the file to produce with it. Stay abreast of current rulings for briefs and letters produced as "native files" (the original Word document, for example), as at least one state considers it unethical to look further than on the surface.[19]

SCENARIO: You've been supplying your opponent with TIFF's and a load file for the last several months. They've been beating the drum to get the native spreadsheets. You've lost the motion and are ordered to produce the spreadsheets. OK, if they want spreadsheets, they will get spreadsheets. But, they won't get any protected information, such as social security numbers. Hmmm. Redacting native spreadsheets is easy. All you need to do is erase the cell contents. Hey, what about the formulas? The other side could change them. You know a way to erase the formulas in the spreadsheet and leave the numbers nicely in place.[20] Boy, you were sure surprised when the court came back with an order to produce the spreadsheets with metadata and formulas intact.

LESSON LEARNED: If you are the producing party, make sure your production is "reasonable" and does not lend itself to being turned into an unfortunate event. When ordered to produce native files, consider very carefully any alteration, like erasing formulas or scrubbing metadata. Scrubbing metadata could be seen as spoliation. Make sure the original dates on the file are intact or produced in a separate reference file.

Make sure you've reviewed for privilege, perhaps by searching the potential production forensically. Remember, hidden columns and password-protected files can be opened and may not be visible in your review application, depending on how the data was processed. Produce the native files, if necessary, on clean or unused media, with a hash of the entire production and each file, so you can authenticate evidence if entered against you. Number each file, as you would Bates each page of a production. Make sure your discovery management system records the production.

---

19 FLORIDA BAR PROFESSIONAL ETHICS COMMITTEE PROPOSED ADVISORY OPINION 06-2 (April 10, 2006)

20 Williams v. Sprint/United Mgmt. Co., 230 F.R.D. 640 (D. Kan. 2005)

Common practice is for the producing party to provide TIFFs, PDFs and load files with extracted text, with follow-up requests for native files on an exception basis. The 2006 FRCP amendments allow the requestors to specify the form(s) of production. The same data is not required to be produced in more than one form. This may limit double dipping for the same data, but it also may increase the initial requests for native productions.[21]

---

21 FRCP 34 (b) (ii) and FRCP 34 (b) (iii)

CHAPTER 2

Why Is e-Discovery Important?

A number of drivers are creating a dramatic increase in the use of e-discovery services.

The most significant is the explosive growth in electronic data. According to recent estimates published in Law Technology News, at least 93% of business documents are created electronically and more than 35% of corporate communications never reach paper.[22]

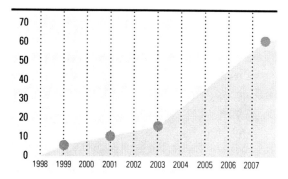

http://www.sims.berkeley.edu/research/projects/how-much-info 2003/internet.htm

The prevalence of e-mail as a primary form of corporate communication adds to the enormity of electronic documents in

---

22 Source: "How Much Information? 2003" by UC Berkeley's School of Information Management and Systems. October 27, 2003.

use today. Forrester Research estimates that large organizations generate upwards of one million e-mail messages per day.[23]

Another key driver is the widespread need for risk management in today's economy. The heightened scrutiny of corporate activity translates into a corresponding increase in the liability exposure of CEO, president, CFO and other "CXO" positions. This exposure is frequently linked to electronic corporate communications, such as e-mail and associated file attachments. In regulated industries, ensuring compliance and avoiding penalties also hinges upon e-discovery and data archiving or preservation.

A third driver is the FRCP amendments that went into effect on December 1, 2006 and are impacting how e-discovery matters are managed. Key impact drivers include shortened timeframes for being prepared to respond to discovery requests (120 days after federal suits are served), expansion of the data subject to discovery ("electronically stored information" (ESI) is specifically named as a category of discoverable information), and increased burden on a company to understand what evidence is accessible and inaccessible and why. Next, both inside and outside counsel were chilled by the Qualcomm decisions discussed earlier.

Finally, as electronic documents and e-mails become ubiquitous, how a corporation routinely stores or destroys such data becomes increasingly important to potential future litigation. The need for prompt and thorough access to electronic documents is crucial. A poorly thought-out records management policy can result in overly burdensome and costly responses to discovery, as well as in missed evidence and lost metadata that may impact litigation. e-Discovery, as an organized business process, is becoming increasingly important to corporations.

Can e-Discovery Ever Be Ignored?

According to legal cyber expert Joan A. Feldman, "What you don't know can hurt you."[24] This is especially true because fewer and fewer documents ever make it to hard copy. Today, electronic

---

23 e-discovery Bursts Onto The Scene. Forrester Research Report, March 1, 2006. http://www.forrester.com

24 "Essentials of e-Discovery: Finding and Using Cyber Evidence," by Joan E. Feldman, Glasser LegalWorks, 2003.

data – not paper – reveals the complete story.

As e-discovery becomes part of the normal course of federal (and most state) lawsuits, the requirements to request and disclose ESI early in a suit make it more likely that more and more cases will have an e-discovery component.[25]

Moreover, for those familiar with e-discovery, it is clear that electronic content and audit trails reveal much more than their paper counterparts. An electronic file contains easily accessible and highly reliable corporate knowledge, leaves a metadata chronology of key dates, comments between collaborators and, in effect, provides a knowledge map of who knew what and when it became known.

Ignoring electronic forms of evidence – or not knowing how to find, preserve and produce those that are relevant – can seriously impact your litigation strategy and effectiveness.

How Is e-Discovery Different?

The good news and the bad news is that digital evidence is rarely ever "gone" even if a party believes they have deleted a file. Thus it can be discovered. However, specialists in forensic computing are needed to retrieve the data while preserving its metadata and enabling the evidence to stand up in court.

Copying files from one device to another for 'review' opens the door to an authenticity challenge for key evidence.

Because ESI can be exchanged, copied, forwarded and modified so freely by individuals other than the original owner, demonstrating chain of custody becomes a crucial issue.

How ESI is stored, as active files or on backup tapes, desktop computers, mobile devices, servers or handhelds, affects the procedures and costs involved in retrieving evidence. It's not as straightforward as requesting "all e-mails" or asking for old-fashioned banker's boxes stuffed with memos.

There are technical issues. Review platforms differ in how they organize data. Can the system match the fields and scale to

---

25 FEDERAL RULES OF CIVIL PROCEDURE - FRCP Rule 16(b) Pretrial Conferences; Scheduling and Planning; FRCP Rule 26(f). General Provisions Governing Discovery - Conference of Parties; Planning for Discovery.

receive the data provided by a respondent? Can it accept electronic documents in a variety of formats? Does data "flow" into a format that can be readily culled, reviewed, protected for privilege and categorized? We'll go into these and other technical issues later, as well as describe how to prepare for e-discovery.

In a nutshell, while ESI is fair game for discovery, the traditional, paper-based discovery procedures do not readily translate to the digital paradigm.[26]

The process of e-discovery may seem overwhelming, but as we've shown, there are significant legal risks if you try to avoid the process altogether. Navigating the seemingly complex maze of the e-discovery process does not have to be difficult. Nor is it recommended, or even possible for any but the few corporations or law firms with an expert e-discovery practice, to do it all alone – any more than you would be expected to forego the use of other experts, such as forensic accountants or expert witnesses, to make your case. e-Discovery can be manageable when you or your partners are familiar with the process.

The importance of accountability – Office of Technology Counsel (OTC)

While e-discovery can be half of the enterprise's legal spend, it is only recently that corporations have appointed one person to be responsible for the process. Sometimes the accountability is assigned to a Director of e-Discovery; sometimes senior counsel, staff attorney, paralegal, manager or IT member on loan to legal. It is rare for this person to have direct reports or to be full time. Some organizations manage the process by consensus.

In order to avoid sanctionable lapses in process and communication, it is essential that one person/department own the accountability for the e-discovery process. Once the process is tamed, it is equally essential for that accountability to go upstream and influence technology purchases and new lines of business by articulating what content needs to be kept, and for how long. Legal holds are a legal requirement and now a business necessity, so why not consider them from the beginning?

---

26 Disinterring the Inaccessible and Intangible; The Fundamental Challenge of e-Discovery," by Dean Gonsowski, J.D., C.I.S.S.P. Trial Talk, August/September 2003.

The OTC should have someone well versed in e-discovery, technology and evidence, with budgeting and management skills. The OTC should have accountability for tactical and strategic matters around e-discovery for all of the enterprise's e-discovery. This will require high level communication skills and the ability to align legal goals with business and technical imperatives.

Most organizations currently have a "virtual" Office of Technology Counsel, where the key contributors work for other people, in other departments. The Technology Counsel or Director of the Office of Technology Counsel will need an executive mandate and collaboration skills to be able to count on people reporting to others.

The importance of collaboration and trust

While trust has been a critical component of successful e-discovery through its early years, it is now a necessity. The amended FRCP establish a collaborative structure for opponents to agree upon some of the tactical decisions around e-discovery, like format of production, preservation issues, cost allocation and privilege handling, to name a few. This requires a special kind of collaboration inside an adversarial process.

Those collaborating, sharing information and making agreements must trust and have the trust of their teams if their information is to be grounded in reality. Without trust, and structures to support efficient and truthful information flow, e-discovery "teams" can get bogged down in wishful thinking, resulting in sanctions or having e-discovery disputes and missteps taint the presentation on the merits.

It is often wise, especially for serial litigants, to formally charter a team that extends across inside counsel, outside counsel, IT, litigation support and key service providers. Having regularly scheduled meetings gets the ordinary handled and makes room for the extraordinary. The person facilitating this meeting (from the Office of Technology Counsel), should be able to draw out all of these constituencies with their varied communication styles and vocabularies. They should be a skilled consensus builder with the ability to be directive when the situation warrants. The environment should support truth telling, no matter how ugly. Ideally, truths would be expressed orally, with resolutions framed in writing.

It is often non lawyers who see the flaw in a process or bring up the uncomfortable issues. Lawyers must learn to set aside their tendency to "shred the witness" and listen for the heart of the matter. When mistakes are made, welcome the news. Better to have it early to be able to rectify and frame how it looks before it blows up unexpectedly. Make sure your processes have quality checks so mistakes can be noted early. Many a sanction could have been avoided had there been effective communication.

With the explosion of e-discovery, finding skilled staff, particularly staff that understands the business of the law firm or organization is invaluable. Working in an adversarial system like litigation can be hard on people, even when their own organization tries to be collaborative. It is important to nurture the career development and other key factors of satisfaction for those in the trenches. Currently, there is always a recruiter at the door ready with greener pastures.

The consequences of communication failures can be severe. The latest example is Qualcomm v Broadcom, where communication apparently broke down between junior and senior attorneys, trial counsel and e-discovery counsel, paralegals and outside counsel, and witness and outside counsel. Establishing formal discovery processes is one way to guard your "good faith." Equally important is the ability to cross hierarchies and organizational borders to raise uncomfortable issues. The client sets the tone. If the client wants the truth, the client will not punish counsel for bringing it. If the client wants collaboration, the client will not allow competing service providers to undermine the other's work or motives. The time for competition is prior to the award for the work on the case. Once chosen, competitors must become collaborators. If they don't, it is much more likely that the client will suffer the results.

CHAPTER 3

How Do You Gain a Strategic Advantage?

Just as individuals are affected in varying ways by e-discovery, so are specific legal areas. The following sums up the strategies that can help bolster your position, depending on the kind of matter and what your area of responsibility might be.

Class Actions

Class actions traditionally originated in state courts where electronic evidence was not very well understood by the judge. Now, after the Class Action Fairness Act, more class actions are originating in Federal Court. As such, plaintiff's attorneys will most likely depose the IT department of their target early in the process to try to get the target on record as destroying evidence in the normal course of business. It is important to play your best game from the beginning, including:

▶ **Do not appear to have something to hide.** For example, continuing with "standard policy" 30-60 day cutoffs on e-mail retention or overwriting tape backups can be perceived as deliberately destroying evidence. Once litigation becomes a possibility, the preservation obligation kicks in. See the discussion regarding legal holds in the chapter on Preservation.

▶ **Consider the jurisdiction.** Forum shopping by plaintiffs looking for the most advantageous venue may find you in court with a judge who knows nothing or absolutely everything about ESI. Find an e-discovery partner with experts who can speak plain language rather than jargon to the judge and who can assist you in tailoring your motions to meet the needs of the specific jurisdiction. Even though the Class Action Fairness Act will bring most e-discovery under Federal Rules, pre-certification discovery can still impact at the state level.

▶ **Make sure you are up on the state rules.** Do not expect all courts to follow one standard. Get familiar with the local rules. Delaware, California and New York have some interesting twists for the e-discovery process.[27]

▶ **Prepare for varying data collection requirements.** You may have special data collection or production requirements by state. Identify and track your custodians by department, project and state from the beginning.

▶ **Plan for the long run.** Class actions drag on. In anticipation, always have in place a data retention plan for departed employees.

▶ **Reduce redundancy** and multiple response strategies. Identify your core custodians early for the class action. Collect them once and produce them often.

▶ **Use keyword search and conceptual analysis,** or concept-based searching, to identify keywords related to the matter. Keyword search is the traditional method used by attorneys to analyze and review ESI. Concept-based search enables legal teams to review the potential evidence by a concept or issue vs. just a keyword. This methodology can help identify better keywords or "smoking guns" that may not have been visible before. Measure the impact of keywords prior to negotiating them with an interplay of concepts backed up by keyword.

▶ **Establish regular collection windows** for easier tracking and less impact on the client's IT department. This is necessary

---

27 http://www.e-discoverylaw.com/2008/01/articles/resources/updated-list-local-rules-forms-and-guidelines-of-united-states-district-courts-addressing-e-discovery-issues/

because class action reviews tend to expand. You may need to refresh the collection the next year, and you'll want to direct the collection team to collect only new data.

▶ **Meet regularly with the IT department and records managers.** Assess who will make the best witness at the deposition. This may not be the e-mail administrator (who can provide hair-raising details of how e-mail is lost on a regular basis). Instead, you may want the highest level person to be deposed, with the preparation for the deposition facilitated by outside counsel or consulting experts. Make sure your witnesses are shielded from strategy discussions.

▶ **Track what has been produced to each requesting party.** Make sure you are prepared to produce the same thing to other parties, depending on the jurisdiction requirements. Don't try to hold back. There are websites selling CDs full of produced evidence, protective orders or not. Inadvertently holding something back in one jurisdiction can impact your case nationally. Make sure your protective orders have teeth to reduce evidence sharing.

▶ **Limit unnecessary multiple or redundant reviews.** You will probably be working with many outside counsel. Make sure there is only one privilege review for each custodian, with a validation step for other litigation. Producing a privileged item in one jurisdiction may cause you to lose the privilege in another jurisdiction.

▶ **Stay flexible and engage a partner.** Find an experienced e-discovery partner with flexible production options. Early on, you will need to produce to a multitude of different law firms, each with their own software needs for reviewing your production. The shift in the FRCP rules to specifically allow requesting parties to specify production format[28] has the potential for your team to need to produce to Concordance, Summation, Ringtail as well as natively for lawsuits involving the same custodians. At some point, lead counsel will be appointed and a general repository or production standard for all law firms may be required. Central management of that repository is recommended.

---

28 FRCP Rule 34(b) - requesting party "may specify the form or forms in which electronically stored information is to be produced."

Second Requests

By their very nature, second requests are on a short deadline and put you in a defensive position. Corporations that are of a certain size who intend to merge or spin off must, by law, file information with the appropriate government agency, usually the Department of Justice or Federal Trade Commission. This is the silent "first request." The governmental agency has a certain number of days (generally 30) to determine if they need more information to green light the transaction. This is when the "Second Request" appears. Second requests follow the rules of the agency that has jurisdiction, such as the Department of Justice or Federal Trade Commission, and are flavored by the perspective and experience of the particular investigator.

The requesting agency generally uses the same boilerplate over and over with a few additions based on industry or knowledge of the companies involved. This forms the foundation for negotiations to begin narrowing the scope of the request. They generally make a first "kitchen sink" request that can be dramatically narrowed by knowledgeable and experienced counsel. There is usually no time to go it alone unless you have a lot of e-discovery experience and the dedicated resources to pull it off. So, be proactive in anticipation of the worst. For most of us, second requests mean:

▶ **Before the deal is done, choose an e-discovery partner.** Create a mock case and send a non-involved, low-level custodian's e-mail box to the vendor as a sample, so as not to expose your pending transaction. Train your discovery team in the review tool you will use in your second request. Establish the data flow to and from your potential partner. Keep your strategy safe and in your pocket by doing this early.

▶ **Do not wait until the second request arrives to begin collecting ESI.** Of course, you will want to argue burden, cost and reasonableness. However, ESI in the wild takes time to collect. Identify your key custodians and begin collecting from the desktops anyway. Remember, executives with laptops will need a non-intrusive time to have data collected.

▶ **Read the request carefully.** Some recent requests required "create and access" dates to be maintained as metadata, which impacts how data is to be collected. Unless that requirement is negotiated away, it mandates evidence quality collection methods rather than simple drag and drop. Consider early collection using evidence quality protocols to make this a non-issue. Ask your e-discovery partner for a project plan that works backward from your desired production date. Estimate volumes and pages/reviewer to determine what level of bulk categorization, duplicate review and incorporation of conceptual strategy is required to meet your time and substantial compliance needs.

▸ **Negotiate what to produce first.** Active, centralized, server-based data is the fastest to collect and therefore to review. Negotiate a protocol that has e-mail, home and shared directories as a first production; desktops and laptops as a secondary production; and archived data as a very distant third. You may be able to narrow the scope of custodians and date ranges through this process.

▸ **Obtain a critical mass of custodian data in a review tool to allow concept searching.** Concept searching, or contextual searching, goes beyond keyword searching and can even generate appropriate keywords, all to help minimize effort while maximizing potentially responsive results. Test the keywords on a sample set of data. Use the keywords in negotiations and/ or to demonstrate that the time period is too broad. Use this documentation to demonstrate your "substantial compliance."

▸ **Negotiate the form of production early.** Waiting until the end can add days to the production date. Printing to hard copy, for example, can delay your compliance by days. With paper bound regulators, some second request participants have negotiated the electronic data first, while maintaining the option of dealing with the paper later. They rarely choose paper. Do not assume the requesting agency will love the idea of your producing native files as they will need to do something with the files before reviewing them.

▸ **Negotiate clear guidelines on what is considered fair game.** For example, chat (instant messages) is not normally collected. Some chat, however, is being retained by financial firms. Chat can be recorded by opponents to your transaction. Take a measure and determine the importance of chat. Other evidence sources that should be negotiated include third-party e-mail (like Yahoo and Hotmail), home computers, Personal Digital Assistants (PDAs), cell phones, flash drives, archived backup tapes, proprietary databases and more. It is usually the quasi-criminal agencies that are interested in these items, not the FTC or DOJ looking for substantial compliance for a commercial transaction.

▶ **Inventory your backups.** Know what you have and be able to prove it and produce it. This can be accomplished by either a physical inventory or an electronic catalog, which is much less expensive than a full restore of each tape. Negotiate for the tape (archival) data to be produced last. As productions and negotiations continue, concentrate on reducing the time period for which production is required. This will dramatically reduce restore and de-duplication charges. On the other hand, restoring, de-duplicating, reviewing and producing targeted archival (tape) data can make you appear extremely compliant and diligent.

▶ **Make sure your e-discovery partner has experience with second requests.** If they do not know what a "spec number" is, for example, take a pass. Spec number is short for specification number. The government has a standard template they use as the kitchen sink for second requests, with each area designated by spec number. They used to demand production by spec number. More often now, production is allowed "in the course of business," which usually means by custodian or department, the way most data is collected.

Intellectual Property Disputes

There are two sides when litigation arises over intellectual property (IP), so we will delineate the perspective from the viewpoint of both sides.

Your company has been accused of stealing secrets.

Your VP of Sales has been crowing about recruiting a key sales person from your fiercest competitor. He cleared the hiring with Human Resources around the issues of territory and non-compete. Now, the competitor has filed suit asking a court to allow their expert to inspect your entire network to confirm that your new hire did not purloin their confidential information.

Meet with opposing counsel and consider using a neutral third-party. Many firms have found themselves in the predicament of trying to prove a negative. They are accused of having a client list, drawings, plans or budgets. As such, the opposition will most likely want to inspect your systems. Even if the firms involved in the dispute are not competitors, no company wants hostile parties combing through their live systems. Have the opponent provide a third-party expert with the files showing the intellectual property believed stolen. Allow the neutral third-party to collect an appropriate subset from your system. For example, one case was settled on favorable terms when there were no file names in common. Another needed to digitally fingerprint each file (hash) for the accused and the accuser and do a comparison. Finding only one file in common, a shareware program, facilitated a settlement. Others required experts to review both sets of documents looking for similarities beyond an exact copy.

The following are actionable strategies to discuss, in light of your particular circumstance and risk level. with your legal counsel:

▶ **Be prepared to prove a negative.** When hiring from a competitor, anticipate an accusation. Assess the risk with the help of counsel. Set aside the earliest backup tape you have outside of the regular rotation to establish your client list and product plans prior to hiring this individual to preserve the data of the key departments.

▶ **Counsel the new hire and his/her new coworkers regarding the conditions of hire.** Document and confirm the conditions of the new employee hire (e.g., not bringing in any client lists, work product and any other confidential information or trade secret).

▶ **Train IT and put a procedure in place** to schedule any transfer of data from your new hire's machine to your company machine for a few days later than the request. Trigger a notification to inside counsel of the request and make sure they sign off before any transfer of data on to a new machine for the new hire. Make sure everyone – human resources, IT, the hiring group, and coworkers – understands the priority and need for these safeguards.

▶ **Isolate the new hire's backups.** While this is not the ideal position to be in, you can minimize risk by giving the new employee brand-spanking new equipment. As a proactive measure, consider creating a separate backup media for the new hires until you are certain you will not be sued. Check in periodically with your new hires to make sure they are complying with their agreement.

▶ **Inquire regarding participation in standards bodies or open source projects.** These may preclude your new hire from working on certain projects.

You believe your ex-employee has taken company secrets to a competitor.

Now imagine the shoe is on the other foot. How can you process the legal landscape so you can prove, if you unfortunately have to, that an ex-employee has made off with intellectual property or confidential company information?

▶ **Make conditions of hire and continued employment clear** and specific from the beginning. Upon hire, have employees sign a statement that they are not allowed to bring other companies' IP into your company or remove any from yours. Draw your non-compete, trade secret and confidentiality conditions narrowly. Specify penalties for non-compliance. Make sure there is a record of any home computer that may be used for work purposes.

▶ **Train managers** in the art of firing people or facilitating a voluntary departure. Make sure there is a culture of treating people fairly. Counsel people before firing them. Let the person go at the end of the day. As you are releasing the person, have IT document taking their equipment from their work area.

▶ **Secure the recovered equipment** so it is not quickly redeployed. Have the network administrators take a snapshot of the home directories and e-mail files. Instruct the e-mail administrator to undelete any e-mails before the snapshot, a secret feature of leading enterprise e-mail platforms. Ask the employee to return any material they brought home to the human resources or legal office and to sign an exit statement that they no longer have any material, along with their original non-compete agreement attached. Explain and document your expectations that they will not carry material to their new employer and let them know you will be contacting the other company's counsel to reiterate that expectation.

▶ **Put the receiving company on notice.** Send a letter with your expectations of the employees behavior, particularly around computerized information.

▶ **Forensically analyze the computers** and all media recovered, just in case unsanctioned sharing activity has already commenced.

▶ **Look for evidence of mass deletions via forensics.** This often indicates a server dump, most often burned to CD or e-mailed via third-party e-mail to a home computer. A claim of a "broken computer" also indicates foul play as does a reformatted hard drive. Data can be recovered from reformatted hard drives. It is important not to ask IT to just "look at the e-mail and files" because doing so will affect the chain of custody record, triggering dates on files to appear as if they were accessed or changed after the employee left.

▶ **Consider special handling for production of source code.** If software code theft is at issue, consider the impact of producing the code electronically. It could be altered enough to not be a copyright violation and then be recompiled. Newer programming platforms even allow source code to be migrated from language to language (such as from C to Visual Studio .NET), obviating copyright claims. Instead, consider making the source code available in a searchable review tool, without offering download or batch print capability. Producing to paper will force your opponent to scan it, putting it right back in electronic form. Consider engaging a software forensics expert who can read code in many languages to testify as to the similarities of the programs.

▶ **Analyze the network and print logs.** Developers, by the nature of their digital savvy, may think they can cover up the electronic trail of any theft. But consider this hypothetical scenario in which even they can be discovered: A hapless programmer is clever enough to not copy his code from his computer to a removable media or to e-mail. Instead, he thinks he is covert to only print out a hardcopy of it. The evidence can still be traced via the company's print server logs, which records file names and the users who send print jobs.

CHAPTER 4

Who Pays For e-Discovery?

Opportunities for Cost Shifting

One way that e-discovery differs from traditional discovery is in the sheer volume, technical issues and costs involved in recovering data, especially for archived data.

This difference has heightened court awareness and sensitivity to questions of what constitutes undue burden. For example: What information is worth disinterring? Who should pay for its production?[29] If you are cognizant of the issues and are prepared, you should be able to take advantage of cost shifting for e-discovery.

Common law, particularly the Zubulake decision, has allowed for cost shifting through the years. The 2006 FRCP amendments put forth a procedure or protocol around cost shifting for ESI:

Duty to Disclose; General Provisions Governing Discovery

(b)(2) Discovery Scope and Limits

(B) A party need not provide discovery of electronically stored information from sources that the party identifies

---

29 Zubulake v. UBS Warburg, LLC, No. 02 Civ. 1243 (SAS) (S.D.N.Y. May 13, 2003)

as not reasonably accessible because of undue burden or cost. On motion to compel discovery or for a protective order, the party from whom discovery is sought must show that the information is not reasonably accessible because of undue burden or cost. If that showing is made, the court may nonetheless order discovery from such sources if the requesting party shows good cause, considering the limitations of Rule 26(b)(2)(C). The court may specify conditions for the discovery.

Sedona Principle 2:

When balancing the cost, burden, and need for electronically stored information, courts and parties should apply the proportionality standard embodied in Fed. R. Civ. P. 26(b)(2)(C) and its state equivalents, which require consideration of the technological feasibility and realistic costs of preserving, retrieving, reviewing, and producing electronically stored information, as well as the nature of the litigation and the amount in controversy.

Sedona Principle 13:

Absent a specific objection, party agreement or court order, the reasonable costs of retrieving and reviewing electronically stored information should be borne by the responding party, unless the information sought is not reasonably available to the responding party in the ordinary course of business. If the information sought is not reasonably available to the responding party in the ordinary course of business, then, absent special circumstances, the costs of retrieving and reviewing such electronic information may be shared by or shifted to the requesting party.

The responding party still has the burden of preserving, if that is the only copy of the discoverable ESI. The responding party, though, can identify backup tapes, obsolete equipment and deleted, fragmented files as inaccessible due to the personnel time or cost to obtain them. Make sure you can quantify your burden or cost. Also make sure your identification of the material will pass muster. For example, "20 Digital Linear Tapes (DLT)" might not be descriptive enough. "Twenty DLTs from the time period (e.g. 1/1/2006-present)" is better. Even better would be "20 DLTs from the time period 1/1/2006-present, which contain monthly backups of the e-mail system."

Understand your costs. Make sure you do not ask for a "burden estimate" from your e-discovery partners or vendors. Burden estimates that do not take into account sampling, de-duplication and other current practices around data reduction generally do not look reasonable in the light of day.

While the new FRCP amendments are extremely influential, state courts and government investigations will follow different rules regarding accessibility and cost shifting. No case has surfaced to date where the government paid costs, although they sometimes will consider burden in shaping discovery requests.

Cost shifting and preservation

While cost shifting remains highly discretionary from court to court, Sedona Principles 5 and 7 address the issue of whether and when. Given the volume and costs of e-discovery, the requesting party is required to show why efforts are warranted, rather than the traditional practice of the responding party demonstrating undue burden:[30]

Sedona Principle 5:
The obligation to preserve electronically stored information requires reasonable and good faith efforts to retain information that may be relevant to pending or threatened litigation. However, it is unreasonable to expect parties to take every conceivable step to preserve all potentially relevant electronically stored information.

Sedona Principle 7:
The requesting party has the burden on a motion to compel to show that the responding party's steps to preserve and produce relevant electronically stored information were inadequate.

---

30 The Sedona Principles: Best Practices Recommendations & Principles for Addressing Electronic Document Production. A Project of the October 2002 Sedona Conference Working Group on Best Practices for Electronic Document Retention & Production, March 2003.

There is some chipping away at the preservation obligation. A Florida dissent quoted Marty Redish, the Northwestern School of Law professor and *Erie* Doctrine scholar, on the proposal that the preservation obligation attaches when the document request is received.[31]

Recent case law supports protection of responding parties from undue burden if they have made reasonable and good faith efforts to preserve data.[32] These evolving opinions create opportunities for cost shifting of preservation efforts if you are aware of how to manage your litigation readiness for e-discovery requests. Conversely, if you are the requesting party, your understanding of what constitutes good practice in e-discovery and how to most effectively acquire the relevant ESI, can help minimize costs and protect against undue burden motions by the opposition.

How to Position for Optimal Cost Shifting

When it comes to who bears the cost burden of e-discovery, there is a difference between accessible and inaccessible data.

Accessible data (also known as active or live data) means the documents are available without resorting to costly and time-consuming retrieval operations. Accessible data could reside on servers, desktops, PDAs, optical disks, etc. Because the perception is that no undue efforts are required to make the data available, the producing party is almost always responsible for these costs, unless the request is overbroad.[33]

In contrast, inaccessible data (also known as archival data) or hidden data (e.g., "deleted" files) require special tools and/or the services of forensic experts to be restored. Here, arguments can be made that the requesting party pays.

The Committee notes to FRCP amendment 26(b)(2)(B) demonstrate the influence the Zubulake opinion has regarding cost shifting.

---

31 Martino, et al. v. Wal-Mart Stores, Inc., 908 So.2d 342 (Fla. 2005)

32 Observations on The Sedona Principles," by John L. Carroll, Dean, Cumberland School of Law, Stanford University, Birmingham A; and Kenneth J. Withers, Research Associate, Federal Judicial Center, Washington, DC.

33 From http://discoveryresources.blogspot.com. As reported by Alexander H. Lubarsky, "Many processes and strategies translated seamlessly from the paper world to the electronic world. Overbroad discovery requests did not."

"Appropriate considerations may include:

1. the specificity of the discovery request;

2. the quantity of information available from more readily available sources;

3. the failure to produce information that for some reason is no longer available but one suspects should have been;

4. the likelihood of finding responsive information that cannot be obtained from a more readily available source;

5. predictions as to the importance and usefulness of the requested information;

6. the importance of the issues at stake in the litigation; and

7. the parties' resources."

A MISSED OPPORTUNITY FOR COST SHIFTING.

SCENARIO: A missed opportunity for cost shifting

A Fortune 100 company, knowing it had a potential government investigation looming, requested that its IT security team preserve data as a preventative measure. As experienced users of EnCase,[34] the IT security team collected desktops in both a forensic and "active" (i.e., "live") fashion.

Next, anticipating that ESI for the past year would be requested, they

---

34 A forensics tool made by Guidance Software (www.guidancesoftware.com).

restored a tape backup of data for each of the 12 months, without overwriting or de-duplication. This resulted in a total of 12 tape backups of highly duplicative data on a server, with each month in its own area on the disk. This effort was time consuming and costly and, while implemented with the best intentions of being litigation ready, actually undermined arguments for cost shifting. In fact, the company had transformed inaccessible data into accessible data twice, first by proactively imaging the drives and next by turning the archival (tape) data into active (disk) data.

At last, becoming concerned about the enormity of the data volume, the company asked for estimates and assistance in reducing the vast data set and about cost shifting. Unfortunately, they had already lost their opportunity to argue cost shifting because they restored the archival data on their own volition before being compelled by discovery.

LESSON LEARNED: All parties would have been better served by negotiating the scope and relevance of any ESI before evidence collection began. Courts are increasingly willing to look to a sampling approach to determine whether to restore all or part of a tape library. Courts are also beginning to see tapes as a disaster recovery tool that happens to be caught in litigation, not as reasonable preservation of active ESI. It is possible that the parties could have negotiated that one month's backups be restored for a small set of custodians. That ESI could have been reviewed and the responsive material produced at less than 10 percent of the cost otherwise incurred. The discussions between inside counsel and outside counsel about what to do with the newly restored data exceeded $100,000. Once an e-discovery partner was engaged, de-duplication and other mitigation strategies were employed to reduce the review and production costs. Backup tapes have a high percentage of duplicates, especially if they are full rather than incremental backups.

It's always a judgment call about what to preserve or collect in a forensic manner. In this case, the client had in-house resources, so the collection was not overly expensive. They could still have an argument to shift the costs for the analysis of the material. The risks and cost of managing e-discovery in a crisis mode can be mitigated by education and training, so that legal and IT departments can lessen the risks of managing a lawsuit in a crisis.[35] It is important for the legal and IT teams to begin to communicate as soon as possible, as technology decisions can impact the cost of responding to potential litigation.

A Strategy for Maximizing Cost Shifting for Productions

Courts are not amused by overbroad discovery requests, such as requiring parties to preserve "all" electronic documents or "all" e-mail.[36] Thus, with preparation and foresight, you can maximize your opportunities for cost shifting and burden if you are faced with such a request. Jurists are increasingly looking toward the "reasonableness" of the request (FRCP 26(b)(2)). The following tactics can help build the case for a cost shifting argument:

1. **Inventory.** Know how many and what kind of tapes or media you have. This will allow you to get estimates for restoring and de-duplicating the tapes. You can then submit those estimates with your arguments to demonstrate burden.

2. **Sample.** If the opponent has requested a four-year period, then four time slices may be appropriate for sampling. De-duplicate and review the material on those tapes to demonstrate that there is no responsive material on the tapes. Sample first and review the results before offering it to the requesting party. Know the impact of what you are offering.

3. **Select.** If you have chosen to preserve forensically, preserve broadly and analyze selectively the drives of individuals whom you believe will help your case. Not preserving material that could help your opponent could also prevent you from introducing material that will help your case.

4. **Wait.** You don't have to restore backup tapes just because

---

35 "Taming the Litigation Beast" by Mary Mack, Esq., www.fiosinc.com/articles.html, April 2004

36 http://discoveryresources.blogspot.com. Ibid. As reported by Alexander H. Lubarsky, "a California Court did not only refuse to compel the Defendant to comply but they fined the requesting party for its overbroad discovery demands." Posted Saturday, December 20, 2003.

you have them.[37] Wait until the opponent claims that there is material on the tapes that will impact favorably on their case. The new FRCP amendments recognize backups for disaster recovery rather than a deep cache for litigation. If the opponent requests forensic preservation or production, obtain an estimate to support the cost-shifting argument.

Don't forget reasonableness

Just because you are asked to produce doesn't mean that you automatically need to go into a cost-shifting mode. Remember to weigh the requests against the reasonableness and proportionality rule. You may not need to produce after all or you may be able to demonstrate that producing active data is sufficient.

FRCP Rule 26(b)(2)(C)

....The frequency or extent of use of the discovery methods otherwise permitted under these rules and by any local rule shall be limited by the court if it determines that: (i) the discovery sought is unreasonably cumulative or duplicative, or is obtainable from some other source that is more convenient, less burdensome, or less expensive; (ii) the party seeking discovery has had ample opportunity by discovery in the action to obtain the information sought; or (iii) the burden or expense of the proposed discovery outweighs its likely benefit, taking into account the needs of the case, the amount in controversy, the parties' resources, the importance of the issues at stake in the litigation, and the importance of the proposed discovery in resolving the issues. The court may act upon its own initiative after reasonable notice or pursuant to a motion under FRCP Rule 26(c).

Trends Toward Cost Limitations

At this writing, three trends are emerging to limit e-discovery costs.

First, organizations are getting "litigation ready" so that the higher cost of fire drills can be mitigated. When content is mapped, there is enough time to map case specific issues to content in preparation

---

37 Creating backups is a relatively inexpensive activity. Therefore organizations are likely to do so. Restoring years of backups when faced with litigation is the costly part.

for the FRCP 26(f) "meet and confer" in order to reduce the scope of e-discovery. Better information governance for e-discovery means that less garbage data will be saved, lowering costs.

Second, the Supreme Court in Twombly[38] cited the high costs of e-discovery as part of their reasoning to limit antitrust suits via the FRCP 12(b)(6) Motion to Dismiss with a requirement for tighter fact pleading before a case can proceed to the discovery phase. This will reduce the number of cases, as it has already been cited by hundreds of other non-antitrust cases. Federal Rule of Evidence (FRE) 502 is in its final stages of approval, proposed and supported in Congress by both parties, in part to reduce privilege review costs.

Third, technology, process and people are combining to reduce preservation and review costs via better archiving, better information governance and better use of professional services. For example, first pass review is becoming a standard where lower cost service providers accomplish the first pass, leaving "polishing the jewels" to the more seasoned, higher cost partners.

---

38 Bell Atlantic Corp. v. Twombly, 550 U.S. ___, 127 S.Ct. 1955, 167 L.Ed.2d 929 (2007).

CHAPTER 5

Ensuring the Preservation of ESI When Litigation is Looming

Evolution of evidence preservation

At one time, capturing and storing business documents was relatively straightforward. Everything was originally in hard copy, whether as formal documents or scribbled notes. Those documents that were deemed to be worth keeping were stored and remained available. Businesses would keep these documents for a specified period of time (or merely until the file cabinets were bulging), then box them up and send them to a storage facility.

In the most structured firms, boxes were numbered and indexed to indicate what they contained, before being shipped to a storage facility. In smaller or more casual businesses, boxes may simply have been stored blind (i.e., no destruction index) at a local warehouse. This was not an "enterprise" undertaking as we understand the term today, but at least it was a methodology that worked most of the time.

If litigation arose, any extant boxes could be retrieved and physically searched for responsive material. The point here is that relevant evidence was easy to determine. In the reality of those days, you simply asked the actors involved, and they pointed you to the relevant filling cabinet or box stored offsite. Most litigation was never more than a few copy boxes and only rarely did you need to do anything besides look it over.

Tedious and time consuming, perhaps. Not to mention the paper cuts. But it was nothing compared to what we have now in the "electronic age." ESI may eventually become evidence. But do you have to save everything? And if so, where?

Sedona Principle 3:
Parties should confer early in discovery regarding the preservation and production of electronically stored information when these matters are at issue in the litigation and seek to agree on the scope of each party's rights and responsibilities.

Sedona Principle 4:
Discovery requests for electronically stored information should be as clear as possible, while responses and objections to discovery should disclose the scope and limits of the production.

But I'm not a records management expert!

What is a record and how long do I have to keep it?
Records that are electronic can exist in many different formats and locations, and like rabbits, keep replicating. A record can also be a conventional document in hard copy. In today's digital age, hard copy may be scanned and captured electronically as well.

Preserving these documents has become a critical business task for today's companies – yet the way they are retained for compliance purposes is dramatically different from how documents must be preserved for litigation. For example, the SEC adopted Rule 2-06 to implement Section 802 of the Sarbanes-Oxley Act, which imposes various retention requirements on publicly traded companies and imposes liability on their chief executive and financial officers for violation of such requirements. How long certain records must be retained is controlled. Audit firms must maintain all work papers related to an audit or review for a period of five years, with fines and/or imprisonment for violations. Accountants of securities issuers must retain records relevant to audits or reviews for a period of seven years.

Companies aren't in the business of being records managers or e-discovery experts. They want to (and should) focus on their core business. They should not be managing records simply for fear of litigation but doing it for meeting necessary business objectives. When you have your records in order, improved litigation readiness naturally follows.

Remember that the possibility of litigation and e-discovery does NOT mean a business has to preserve every e-mail, every document or every record forever. Instead, there should be a records management policy in place with standard capture and destruction policies to support business needs, such as compliance audits and everyday operations. The destruction policies need only be suspended for potentially responsive documents when litigation is likely. Additionally, an enterprise-wide taxonomy may be overkill to address future discovery requirements.

Commenting on the recent reversal of the Arthur Anderson decision and the importance of records management, the firm of Fulbright and Jaworski stated:

"As always, the safest way to avoid civil and criminal liability is to follow records management best practices. No corporation that has acted diligently, competently and in good faith has been subject to liability. The market may evolve to the point, as it did in the pharmaceutical industry, that to demonstrate good faith an organization must make appropriate, proactive infrastructure investments to store, retain, and retrieve subject material."

According to Sedona, an appropriate records and information management program would involve most or all of the following.[39]

▶ Establishing an appropriate and workable retention schedule for paper and electronically stored information

▶ Helping business units establish practices and customs, tailored to the needs of their businesses, to identify the business records they need to retain

▶ Addressing the retention of e-mail and other communications, such as instant messaging and voice mail

▶ Addressing other forms of electronically stored information that are created in the ordinary course of business

▶ Developing communications policies that establish and promote the appropriate use of company systems

---

39 http://www.thesedonaconference.org/content/miscFiles/TSC_PRINCP_2nd_ed_607.pdf

▶ Training individuals to manage and retain business records created or received in the ordinary course of business.

Any records program must have a companion policy for legal holds to enforce preservation duties if litigation seems likely. Automation and process is a benefit, but you don't want a records policy where the auto-pilot can't be disabled. However, when litigation becomes likely these routine destruction policies must be suspended for potentially responsive records.

Save what you need to manage the business, but also have a process in place that allows for preservation of files when needed for an anticipated litigation or investigation. The principal advantage of having such a process in place is that when litigation happens, counsel can be quickly directed to where the relevant content can be found. As a result, the discovery practice is expedited with built in processes that will reduce costs and risks at every phase.

Regardless of where your company is on the "litigation readiness" curve, there is still an obligation to preserve. The risks of not having a legally defensible process for preservation and collection in place are high and can result in:

▶ Sanctions by courts or regulatory bodies

▶ Unpredictable costs (unpredictability in terms of cost, time, and risk)

▶ Poor outcomes in litigation

▶ Lack of repeatability – every matter becomes a new fire drill

You don't have to preserve everything

The manager of e-discovery should work with an appointed IT representative in order to fully understand the organization's records management plan. The person should be able to identify the network map, retentions policies and back-up schedules. It is also very important to identify what the company does with data for departed employees.

The whole issue of e-discovery can be scary. Sure, there is more potential evidence to find and derivative sources and volumes of data to consider than ever in the days of plain old paper documents.

On the bright side, the basic rules of the court prevail. According to Laura Kibbe, Esq.:[40]

> "In an attempt to appear informed and on top of our e-discovery game, and in the era of 'Zubulake,' we may have overindulged complexity. e-Discovery conferences abound, service providers purport to provide the hottest new 'tools' for discovery, and lawyers take newly learned jargon into the courtroom. All this misses a very basic tenant of discovery: FRCP 26(a) 'Required Disclosures.' Neither technology nor the proposed amendments can change this basic obligation."

She also notes that while e-discovery is different from traditional discovery, many of the questions remain the same. To ensure companies fulfill their preservation obligations they need to answer some basic questions:

1. What will be the court's (and my opposition's) expectation of what I need to preserve?

2. Do I believe that expectation is fair and defensible?

3. Do I believe my adjustment of their expectation is defensible?

4. Can I ensure that the actions I take to identify potentially responsive evidence will demonstrate good faith?

5. Can I ensure the processes I use to preserve evidence will maintain the evidence in an un-altered state?

6. Can I ensure that I know exactly where the evidence has been and who has accessed or interacted with it?

7. Can I demonstrate I have taken proactive steps to cease the (normal course of business) destruction of documents in order for them to be preserved?

8. Do I believe that the (imminent) discovery request will be overly burdensome for me to respond to?

---

40 From "WYSIWYG...Your Honor," by Laura Kibbe, Esq. Corporate Counsel Magazine, June 2005

The 2006 Amendments to the Federal Rules of Civil Procedure do not specially spell out when or how a preservation obligation with respect to e-mail is triggered nor do they identify the exact scope of the duty and how it is to be satisfied. Parties are instead encouraged by Rule 26(f) to assess and discuss preservation issues early and Rule 37(e) provides for limited protection from some spoliation sanctions based on the presence of "routine, good faith" operations of information systems .**41**

The origin of the duty to preserve potential evidence arose from the common law, with courts establishing local rules for digital evidence – "Duty to Investigate and Disclose. Prior to a Fed. R. Civ. P. 26(f) conference, counsel shall review with the client the client's information management systems, including computer-based and other digital systems, in order to understand how information is stored and how it can be retrieved. To determine what must be disclosed pursuant to Fed. R. Civ. P. 26(a)(1), counsel shall further review with the client the client's information files, including currently maintained computer files as well as historical, archival, backup, and legacy computer files . . ." District of New Jersey, Local Rule 26.1(d)(1)**42**

The 2006 amendments to FRCP Rule 37(e) created a "safe harbor" inducement to properly preserve:

> "Electronically stored information. Absent exceptional circumstances, a court may not impose sanctions under these rules on a party for failing to provide electronically stored information lost as a result of the routine, good-faith operation of an electronic information system."

While this rule may seem to excuse overwriting, it is not intended to gut preservation obligations. Further, it imposes a "good faith" and "routine" standard of behavior around IT systems operations. Document retention policies and audits to assess and increase compliance with them should be part of a risk reduction strategy. Document retention (destruction) policies followed only after a

---

41 http://www.thesedonaconference.org/content/miscFiles/Commentary_on_E-mail_ Management___revised_cover.pdf

42 See the Fios webcast for more information. "Creating a Defensible and Credible Evidence Preservation/Collection Plan in the Face of Impending Litigation," http://www. fiosinc.com/events/webcast_archive.html

litigation trigger will not demonstrate good faith. Notes to FRCP 37(e) specifically state:

> "Good faith may require that a party intervene to modify or suspend certain features of the routine operation of a computer system to prevent the loss of information, if that information is subject to a preservation obligation...."

This rule does give an enterprise breathing room around transactional databases and other automatic purging systems during the early stages of litigation. However, it would be unwise to stretch this rule to keep on overwriting e-mails and backup tapes without assessing the risks for that particular litigation. The notes say:

> "A party is not permitted to exploit the routine operation of an information system to thwart discovery obligations by allowing that operation to continue in order to destroy specific stored information that it is required to preserve."

The duty to preserve exists even in the absence of a preservation letter or order. Unfortunately, the "trigger" of that duty is often unclear, and it may apply at any of several stages.

So how do you decide what to do without over preserving? Remember if you over-preserve you risk adding more processing, reviewing and production time, as well as reduce your ability to argue cost-shifting and burden. A balancing test considers the following three factors when deciding a motion to preserve documents:

1. The level of concern the court has for the continuing existence and maintenance of the integrity of the evidence in question in the absence of an order directing preservation of the evidence

2. Any irreparable harm likely to result to the party seeking the preservation of evidence absent an order directing preservation

3. The capability of an individual, entity, or party to maintain the evidence sought to be preserved, not only as to the evidence's original form, condition or contents, but also

the physical, spatial and financial burdens created by
ordering evidence preservation[43]

Although negligent e-discovery conduct has been sanctioned
in all 12 federal judicial circuits,[44] a survey by Judge Scheindlin
indicates that the sanctions aren't arbitrary nor imposed for honest
mistakes. "The results of our survey reveal that the profile of a
typical sanctioned party is a defendant that destroys electronic
information in violation of a court order, in a manner that is willful
or in bad faith, or causes prejudice to the opposing party.[45]

It is important to consult local rules in order to verify that there is not
specific language that further defines duty to preserve. For instance,
some courts have concluded that defendants' duty to preserve was
triggered by specific events, such as filing of complaint, and not
by earlier demand letters.[46] Fortunately, while the duty to preserve
evidence is a broad mandate, it does not require a litigant to keep
every scrap of paper or electronic document. Moreover, in some
circumstances, information searches can be easily automated.

"[If it is not feasible to speak with every key player] counsel
must be more creative. It may be possible to run a system-wide
keyword search; counsel could then preserve a copy of each
'hit.' Although this sounds burdensome, it need not be."[47]

A caveat about preservation orders: Do not rely solely on
the cooperation of employees. One of the primary reasons
that electronic data is lost is ineffective communication with
employees and information technology personnel. It is imperative
that companies consider the impact of e-mail on its litigation.

According to records management expert Charlene Brownlee,
every employee is now a records manager because of the

---

43 Capricorn Power Company, Inc. v. Siemens Westinghouse Power Corporation, Civil
Action No. 01-39J, 2004 WL 870659 (W.D. Pa. April 21, 2004).

44 "The e-Discovery Missteps that Judges Love to Hate," by Paul Neale, Law Practice
Today, February 2005

45 Shira A. Scheindlin and Kanchana Wangkeo, e-Discovery Sanctions in the Twenty-
First Century,11 Mich. Telecomm. Tech. L. Rev. 71 (2004), available at http://www.mttlr.
org/voleleven/scheindlin.pdf

46 Cache La Poudre Feeds, LLC v. Land O' Lakes, Inc., 2007 WL 684001 (D. Colo. Mar.
2, 2007),

47 Zubulake v. UBS Warburg, LLC, 2004 WL 1620866 (S.D.N.Y. July 20, 2004)

proliferation of electronic communications.[48] As a result of this fact, you can never rely entirely on technology to determine whether an e-mail is a record. Employees must be trained on what constitutes a record and how that record must be saved in accordance with the organization's records retention schedule. A well-intended policy means nothing if not properly enforced. Communication with the impacted employees is imperative. If data needs to be collected from an employee, that person should fully understand the nature of the litigation hold.

Risk Management: E-mail

In the paper world, all content could become evidence. Therefore, it was usually categorized or indexed, as discussed above. The problem with e-mail is that the content resides on people's "in" boxes, PDAs, network file shares and multitudes of other non-categorized locations. As a result the amount of effort to find relevant ESI has increased remarkably. Additionally, people now put comments into electronic communication that they would never have put in a paper memo – the filters of the paper systems are gone. This free-wheeling activity has opened many a corporation to unprecedented liability (i.e. Zubulake).

Even government organizations are not above making critical errors in recovery and preservation programs. White House officials have acknowledged in press and congressional briefings that e-mail was missing from the White House archive, and that the EOP, in 2002, abandoned the electronic records management system previously put in place. Whistleblowers, cited in conjunction with a Freedom of Information Act lawsuit brought by the watchdog group Citizens for Responsibility and Ethics in Washington (CREW), have alleged that more than 5 million e-mail messages were missing from the White House servers.[49]

Although the outcome of this case is yet to be determined at the time of this writing, it exemplifies how e-mail preservation and retention are becoming easy targets for cases involving document mishandling.

---

48 "The Challenge of Electronic Records: Corporate Compliance — From E-mail to I-Pods," By Charlene Brownlee and Melissa Cozart. June 2005 edition of the LAW JOURNAL NEWSLETTERS - THE CORPORATE COUNSELOR. ALM Properties, Inc.

49 http://www.gwu.edu/~nsarchiv/news/20070905/index.htm

In Intel v. AMD[50], AMD claims Intel used a "move it or lose it Honor System" for preservation and as a result, lost key e-mail when its automatic deletion sweep occurred. Intel continues to defend its good faith in getting its corporate arms around a global preservation for 1,000 people. Making sure 1,000 people archive not only their potentially relevant inbox items, but also sent items can be problematic.

The unfolding of this case underscores the need to not only to demonstrate good faith, but to document the good faith as preservation is occurring. These cases are just a few examples that demonstrate the trend of increased scrutiny of e-mail preservation by the courts.

Sedona has provided some guidelines on e-mail policy development s follows:[51]

Guideline 1: E-mail retention policies should reflect the input of functional and business units through a team approach and should include the entire organization including any operations outside the United States.

Guideline 2: The team should develop a current understanding of e-mail retention policies and practices actually in use within the entity.

Guideline 3: An entity should select features for updates and revision of e-mail retention policy with the understanding that a variety of possible approaches reflecting size, complexity, and policy priorities are possible.

Guideline 4: Any technical solutions should meet the functional requirements identified as part of policy development and should be carefully integrated into existing systems.

E-mail archiving programs:
It is important to address the differences between archiving and back-up data.

With most archive solutions available on the market, as e-mail

---

50 In Re Intel Corp. Microprocessor Antitrust Litig., 2008 WL 2310288 (D.Del. June 4, 2008)

51 http://www.thesedonaconference.org/content/miscFiles/Commentary_on_E-mail_ Management___revised_cover.pdf

and instant messages are sent and received, each message is bifurcated and copied into the archive before it reaches the Exchange, Notes, or Groupwise e-mail server, or whatever instant messaging infrastructure is in use. Message integrity needs to be maintained to avoid spoliation concerns, and all messages end up in the archive. An archive has a broad impact on the overall corporate IT infrastructure, as can be seen in Figure 3 below.[52]

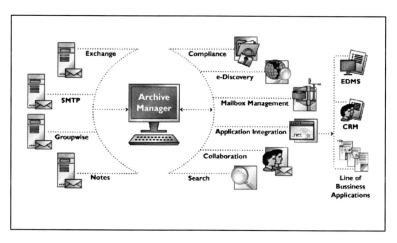

Figure 3: *Archival in the Corporate IT Ecosystem – Courtesy of Quest Software.*

By contrast, this is not the case for daily backups, due to ongoing deletion of messages by users. Backups represent a point-in-time snapshot of e-mail data, but are not intended in any way to provide an archive or compliance solution of any sort. Companies relying on backup media for records management purposes end up having to spend substantial amounts on consulting engagements with forensics experts or on in-house resources using recovery-from-backup solutions to recover e-mail from backups.[53]

Archiving is NOT the same as Disaster Recovery

Non-IT persons should know that there is a difference between backup tapes maintained for disaster recovery and live data. Sedona has addressed this in Principle 8, so that there is no confusion over the fact that how the data is maintained does affect its accessibility.

---

52 From: http://www.edrm.net/wiki/index.php/Records_Management_-_E-Mail_Archiving

53 From: http://www.edrm.net/wiki/index.php/Records_Management_-_E-Mail_Archiving

Sedona Principle 8:

The primary source of electronically stored information for production should be active data and information. Resort to disaster recovery backup tapes and other sources of electronically stored information that are not reasonably accessible requires the requesting party to demonstrate need and relevance that outweigh the costs and burdens of retrieving and processing the electronically stored information from such sources, including the disruption of business and information management activities.

One the main advantages of using a more sophisticated archival system is to allow for quick search and retrieval of known relevant data.

Automating the search for information can minimize the impact of employee noncompliance with legal holds, but counsel must still issue a "litigation hold" at the outset of litigation or whenever litigation is reasonably anticipated. The hold should be periodically re-issued so that new employees are aware of it, and so that it is fresh in the minds of all employees. Counsel should assess compliance with the hold and create a record of good faith by reinforcing the hold. Counsel should communicate directly with the "key players" in the litigation. As with the litigation hold, the key players should be periodically reminded that the preservation duty is still in place.

And once again, all of this becomes easier, more efficient and legally defensible when you have a complete discovery response and preservation plan in place. To make this plan defensible, counsel must now understand what areas of the enterprise are being searched or inventoried, and with what methodology. In Morgan Stanley v. Coleman, the judge was concerned about:

▶ Waves of backup tapes that were not disclosed in a timely manner,

▶ Servers where e-mail archiving was being staged prior to full deployment

▶ Attachments not being searched due to script error

▶ Hits missed by the search engine due to "hyper" case sensitivity (i.e. Coleman would not be a hit if the search term was coleman)

If the costs of preservation are exorbitant, consider requesting or offering to pay or share costs. See Chapter 4 on "Who Pays for e-Discovery" for strategies to shift preservation costs.

Learn from what not to do:

Despite repeated document demands, repeated court orders to produce, and repeated assurances that all appropriate e-mails were being produced, thousands of Health Net's employees' e-mails were never searched. Many others were lost permanently due to Health Net's e-mail retention/non-retention practices, which were only disclosed to the Court after the conclusion of the Rule 37/Integrity hearing. These practices were never disclosed to the Magistrate Judge who supervised discovery for over three years.

Defendants did not inform either Plaintiffs or the Magistrate Judge that e-mails were routinely sent to a back-up tape after 90 days; that employees generally could not search for their own e-mail older than 90 days; that deleted e-mails were lost forever upon transfer to the back-up tape; the numbers of e-mails that needed to be searched; the cost of such a search; or a plan for allocating the burden of e-mail production. If Defendants had candidly disclosed these issues to the Magistrate Judge, an appropriate order could have been tailored to deal with such issues and keep costs down.

The court listed several factors, in roughly their order of importance, to consider when conducting the cost-shifting analysis: the extent to which the request is specifically tailored to discover relevant information; the availability of such information from other sources; the total cost of production, compared to the amount in controversy; the total cost of production, compared to the resources available to each party; the relative ability of each party to control costs and its incentive to do so; the importance of the issues at stake in the litigation; and the relative benefits to the parties of obtaining the information. Cost-sharing options could have been considered at the outset of discovery had Health Net been candid with the Court about their e-mail policies and the expense of producing that discovery. Defendants' lack of candor, however, foreclosed such an approach. Simply put, Health Net did not even tell its outside counsel at McCarter & English about its 90-day back-up tape system for storing e-mail. Therefore, outside counsel conducting discovery did not know, when Health Net's employees were asked to search e-mail, that they could only look through the most recent 90 days.[54]

---

54 Wachtel v. Health Net, Inc., 2006 WL 3538935 (D.N.J. Dec. 6, 2006)

CHAPTER 6

Data Collection: Maintaining the Audit Trail

By now the storm clouds are not just gathering, but the wind is blowing a gale, lightning strikes regularly, and you can feel the thunder. A legal proceeding — litigation or an investigation — is upon you. Yet, if you've completed at least some of the strategic steps outlined in the previous chapters, you are more than ready to weather the squall. The time has come to marshal the resources necessary to collect your data in a responsible, defensible manner.

For a thorough and efficient data collection you must conduct the following activities:

▶ Develop a collection plan

▶ Identify key contacts at your client's site(s)

▶ List all custodians and the location of their data

▶ Identify the sources of data (paper, active, archival, forensic)

▶ Decide who executes the collection

▶ Monitor the collection and chain of custody forms

A little later, we'll offer some factors to consider when deciding whether to collect on your own or engage an experienced partner.

Many businesses are diligent and organized about their primary electronic data storage and backup procedures, which can simplify collection. Yet, at many other companies, especially startups or larger conglomerates that are the product of mergers and acquisition, data is not typically stored or routinely preserved in a documented, predictable manner. Systematically archived and stored data is easier to access and able to flow smoothly into a preservation system structured for legal purposes. Whether a company is diligent or lax about data storage and backup, transitory data, such as e-mails or documents kept on desktop computers, flash drives and PDAs, is always challenging to secure and gather. Fortunately, the complexities of data collection can be easily managed by a competent e-discovery services partner. One of the key areas of value offered by a partner is the staff's experience with like customers, the ability to understand what the bar for success looks like, and their ability to deliver defensible benchmarks and best practices.

To perform comprehensive data collection, you or your e-discovery partner will need to work with your client's records management and IT teams to identify those areas that are of critical interest to your legal team. You should have a technically skilled and articulate data collection team that can collaborate with your client to collect data in a professional manner. Your partner should be able to acquire data in "stealth mode" in the middle of the night, or during regular business hours, depending on the needs of your matter. Collection and preservation methods should take into account personnel resources, capital cost and the necessity of keeping business processes running at optimal levels.

International Collection

Most countries, other than the US, have a bias toward protecting individual privacy. Almost all have rules and laws about cross-border data transfer. Make sure you are working with "Safe Harbor Certified" providers in the U.S. It is critical to work with experienced providers, as a "couple of days" in customs can put a wrench in a review schedule. Although The Sedona Conference has a new working group dedicated to International Electronic Information Management, Discovery and Disclosure, they have not released any publications to date. In January 2008, the group did release the "The Sedona Canada Principles Addressing e-Discovery."

Understanding Data Types and Collection Costs

While negotiating the scope of discovery in the early "meet and confer" stages, you may have already limited the potentially responsive data universe to a certain type of data. The following table outlines the three main types of data and their characteristics:

Data Type	Cost of Collection	Characteristics
Active	Easiest to get, least costly.	Documents that "actively" reside on the custodian's computer hard drive or other storage device. Active documents are generally those that you can see in a file manager or explorer type of tool. Examples include e-mail and standard office documents like word processing and spreadsheets.
		Active files are generally easy to access and collect. Challenges include dealing with large volumes of data and preserving file date information. Most requests for production ask for active files.
Archival	Requires restoration, costs vary on volume and backup	Documents and files stored, often in a compressed format, on off-line devices, including backup tapes or disks, floppies, and optical media. Archived documents are harder and more expensive to retrieve than active documents because they often require restoration, have complex file structures or are on media that can't be accessed at high speeds. Challenges include dealing with old backup formats or tapes that are not cataloged.
		De-duplication is an additional challenge when faced with multiple backups of the same set of data over time.
		Lines are being blurred with the widespread acceptance of "near line" storage where "archives" are written to an online media, for speed of disaster recovery or automatic failover.
		This data is often deemed "not reasonably accessible". Sampling may be helpful for quantifying costs, time and likelihood of non duplicative discoverable data.
Forensic	Most expensive, requires special tools	Documents and files that are hidden or have been erased, fragmented, or damaged, and that can reside on either on-line or off-line storage devices. Forensic collection provides the most detail and is the only approach for retrieving deleted or fragmented files; however it requires an expert to operate special tools and is time consuming.
		Collect forensically when you need maximum preservation protection, such as when you are responding to a specific event like a wrongful termination law suit. Often, the only way to collect data from a PDA is forensically. Due to cost and/or exposure, opposing counsel is usually not willing to provide forensically collected data, but as with archival data, will need to document this burden in the FRCP 26(f) meet and confer conference. Typically, the requesting party will be required to bear the cost of forensic collection.
Legacy	Tools may no longer be available; may need experts	Documents or files contained in very old systems that are no longer in use, but may have been mothballed and still can be turned on. Many systems from prior to Y2K fall into this category. Also data on extremely old media where equipment is no longer common to read them.

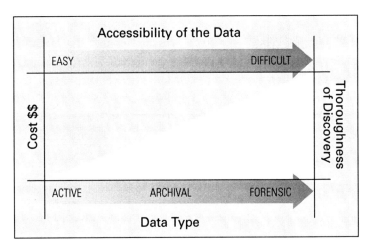

Cost and thoroughness vs. accessibility and data types.

Sedona Principle 9:

Absent a showing of special need and relevance, a responding party should not be required to preserve, review, or produce deleted, shadowed, fragmented, or residual electronically stored information.

Is it Always Necessary to Collect Forensically?

There are many factors to consider before collecting forensically. The legal team will need to assess the case, the jurisdiction, the custodians, data types and the judge to determine whether forensics are warranted. Factors include whether sanctions have already been applied, the trust level for custodians, whether the case is criminal or quasi criminal and other such considerations. The following chart can assist your decision making.

e-Discovery vs. Computer Forensics[55]

Factors	e-Discovery	Computer Forensics
Number of reviewers	Hundreds at a time	One at a time
Location of reviewers	Geographically dispersed	One place
Type of data	Live (unless other data provided by forensics partner)	Live, resurrected, reconstructed fragments
Recover deleted files	No (unless provided by forensics process)	Yes
Recover Web-based e-mail, instant messages	No (unless provided by forensics process)	Possibly
Encrypted and password-protected files	Yes	Yes
Testimony	Fact (protocol)	Opinion (expert)
Who conducts and refines searches	Legal team and/or vendor	Forensic technician
Search time	Minutes	Hours or days
Type of collection	Bit image and/or copy	Bit image only
Downtime of client computers	Sometimes	Usually
Chain of custody forms	Yes	Yes
Special collection tools	Yes	Yes
Testifying expert necessary	Seldom	Often
Cooperation of IT staff	Yes	No
File Listings and structures	Yes	Yes
Metadata	Yes	Yes
Production	Native file, print, Web review, litigation support load files with images and searchable text	Native file, print

Collect the Data

Because distributed data is the norm in today's business environment, you will find that relevant ESI is likely located in different geographic locations and systems, and controlled by many people and departments. For large organizations, the process of data acquisition from multiple office locations and scores of employees can be difficult without the right tools and processes. You'll want to be sure that your team is experienced at

---

55 "e-Discovery and Computer Forensics: The Differences You Need to Know," Legal Tech Newsletter, Volume 21, Number 5 (August 2003)

rapidly identifying and properly collecting large quantities of data from multiple sources.

Maintaining data integrity is critical. If you can't authenticate the data, your legal risks increase and you may not be able to use it at trial. You'll need to be certain that a complete chain of custody for collected data is maintained to ensure accurate and authenticated information. The appendices of this guide provide useful data collection forms to help you document the chain of custody. Be sure that you employ procedures to minimize the risk of damaging, destroying or otherwise compromising evidence during the collection process.

The following activities are crucial for complete and methodical data collection:

▶ Identify stores of data that may fall within the discovery requirements.

▶ Maintain chain of custody for any data that is collected.

▶ Document the source, as well as the rationale, for what data you decide to include in your data set.

▶ Develop a list of all potentially relevant data custodians.

▶ Match actual name (last, first) with ID (employee numbers, usernames, etc.) used by the data or document management systems. You should also review and cross-reference names from prior collections.

▶ Determine the location of data, from sources such as:

- E-mail servers

- File and print servers

- Desktops and onsite laptops

- Field laptops

- Home computers

- Personal Digital Assistants (PDAs)

- Enterprise Document Management or Records Management repositories

- Shared directories

- Backup tapes

- Disks

- CD-ROMs

- DVD-ROMs

- Cell phones

- Flash memory cards such as "thumb drives"

- MP3 players (modern players support storing data)

- iPods

- Voice over IP phone systems

- Instant Messaging

- Online transactions and databases

▶ Work with an infrastructure specialist to set up collection servers at optimum network points.

▶ Use appropriate tools and chain of custody documentation and, when feasible, copy the data over the network to high-speed, removable hard drives. Be aware that doing a straight copy can result in altered metadata; hence you'll want the assistance of an expert in data collection for e-discovery. Regardless of whether the IT department or your e-discovery partner performs the collection, make sure that the tools are used appropriately to maintain metadata and to log for completeness. Common IT tools like Robocopy and exMerge can be used, and are best used with "switches" different from the day to day IT use.

▶ If you use an outside entity, your partner likely will need some assistance to access the appropriate areas of the network and specific drives for security reasons, unless the collection is a black box forensic collection.

▶ If the internal IT team performs data copying tasks, they'll need to securely package the data and send or hand-carry it to your e-discovery partner with chain of custody forms. To maintain chain of custody documentation, your e-discovery partner must properly receive the data.

▶ When collecting traditional voice data files, make sure you work with the telecommunications specialists. They will know how to pull by date, speaker and/or phone number if their software allows it. In order to remain in compliance with SEC Rule 17a-4, financial firms must retain recordings of trading. Other firms employ "audio quality" programs to monitor call center agent performance. There may be exculpatory evidence in these systems. Many proprietary and newer Voice over IP systems save or convert these to recordings as .wav files. These can be searched, reviewed and produced on electronic review systems that allow the download and production of a native file.[56] Unified messaging introduces those .wav files into the e-mail content store.

▶ Collecting huge databases requires consultation with legal and dba's (data base administrators) to make sure that the information is usable by the review team and will not compromise an organization's security or regulatory requirements (like HIPAA). Options include taking a snapshot by saving a daily backup, creating a query and working with the results, or offering up monitored access to a subset of the database via security procedures.

▶ Collecting workflow systems requires collecting both workflow (perhaps screenshots) and the data behind the workflow.

▶ Collecting websites, blogs, wiki's and SharePoint sites requires special tools and procedures for authenticity and chain of custody.

The integrity and quality of your electronic data is clearly of paramount importance. To assist you in proper tracking and documentation during this phase of the e-discovery process, we have included a variety of useful data collection forms in the appendices of this guide.

TIP: Data Collection Efficiency

It is best to do as much live data collection as possible up front rather than having it come in small increments to maintain a "point in time" preservation set and to reduce wear and tear on the collection personnel and custodians. To optimize the data management and culling, it is best to process and review sets of media (such as quarterly backups), rather than one-at-a-time items (such as daily backups). Once your data is collected, your e-discovery partner should be able to rapidly produce documents in rolling deliveries.

---

56 See "Voice Mail and Audio Recordings: Evolving E-Discovery Standards," white paper by Fios, Inc. and Nexidia

With that said, however, there is often an unavoidable incremental nature to data collection. You may have to refresh the data set when new information becomes available. Try to keep these collection events as consolidated as possible to make the process easier and more productive for your client.

There is a school of thought that preservation can occur "in place" and selective collection will reduce downstream costs. Consider the case exposure, potential for issues to change and sophistication of your opponents before employing this strategy. Preservation in place depends on the compliance of the custodians and bears monitoring.

Your e-discovery partner should assist you in tracking collection events.

Can You Collect the Data Yourself?

With proper training, protocols and supervision, the IT staff can directly perform the data collection. Yet often times, you could be faced with these challenges regarding evidence collection:

▶ The case is inappropriate for in house collection (high level internal investigation, IP case where IT is implicated)

▶ Too much data to review

▶ Too costly to collect for legal purposes (burden on IT staff)

▶ Not enough staff to perform actual collection

▶ Risk of your lawyers or IT personnel being called upon to testify as fact witnesses

▶ Can't collect data fast enough (for project timeline)

▶ Don't know how to collect or how to collect responsibly and defensibly (avoiding spoliation, maintaining chain of custody)

▶ Don't know what to collect

▶ Don't know where the data is physically

▶ Don't know how to track a collection project (can't answer the questions, "How much have we collected? How much more do we have to collect? When will we be done collecting?")

▶ Don't know how to manage the security issues for in-house teams accessing sensitive data

▶ The team may inadvertently make biased or prejudiced collection decisions

Risks of Data Collection by Employees

A significant area of risk arises if company employees are allowed to determine which data residing on their computers or storage media is potentially relevant. At this writing, employee self preservation (let alone collection) is being weighed by a court in the AMD/Intel antitrust case. There, employee determined preservation was disdainfully termed the "Honor System" by counsel to AMD. There are multiple problems inherent in employee data selection and collection:

▶ There may be an inconsistent understanding or interpretation among employees as to what constitutes relevancy. If a corporate management team tells 10 of its employees to gather all of their electronic documents related to a specific topic, there will likely be 10 different opinions regarding what is relevant. The attorneys responsible for discovery should clearly define and determine what data is considered relevant, rather than leaving that determination up to the original data custodians.[57]

▶ The lack of a cohesive collection strategy may make the data unreliable. If the data collection activity is too narrow or has the potential for being inconsistent, any changes in the scope or in the issues of the case may drive the need for future rounds of data collection.

▶ Having employees copy their information over to a centralized location creates a significant risk of data alteration resulting from functions that automatically update data within word processing and spreadsheet programs ("AutoSave"), as well as viral exposure.

▶ Employees who are aware of relevant documents within their data sets may be inclined to avoid potential legal risks created by the documents; hence they may inappropriately self-cull the data. Other employees may have embarrassing material that could cause them to cull excessively or delete documents.

---

57 United States of America v. Philip Morris, breaking at publication time (7/21/04), sanctioned the company $2.75 million and 11 employees $250,000 each.

▶ Employees who are involved in the data collection are immediately made fair targets for being called to testify regarding the completeness and accuracy of their data collection.

Data Magnitude Explained

When facing the prospect of data collection, many litigation teams are not yet familiar with the sheer magnitude of data stored on archival systems, servers, hard drives and other storage media. The terms "megabytes," "gigabytes" and "terabytes" are commonly used, but it often is difficult to gage what those data volumes mean in terms of page equivalents. The following conversion table provides a data equivalent overview.

Boxes of Paper	Total Pages	Electronic Equivalent	
1	2,500	50	Megabytes
10	25,000	500	
20	50,000	1	Gigabyte
100	250,000	5	
200	500,000	10	
300	750,000	15	
400	1,000,000	20	
500	1,250,000	25	
1,000	2,500,000	50	
2,000	5,000,000	100	
5,000	12,500,000	250	
10,000	25,000,000	500	
20,000	50,000,000	1	Terabyte
40,000	100,000,000	2	
60,000	150,000,000	3	

After terabytes...?

▶ Comes petabytes and exabytes. A petabyte equals 1,000 terabytes, while an exabyte equals 1,000 petabytes.

▶ All words ever spoken by human beings amounts to about five exabytes.[58]

---

58 "How Much Information?," a study published by SIMS, October 27, 2003. © 2003 Regents of the University of California. Downloadable at: http://www.sims.berkeley. edu/research/projects/how-much-info-2003/

Compared to...?

▶ The complete works of Shakespeare amount to about 5 megabytes.

▶ One terabyte is equivalent to 50,000 trees made into paper

▶ If digitized, the 19 million books and other print collections in the Library of Congress would contain about 10 terabytes of information.

The assumptions for this exhibit are that the average banker's box holds 2,500 sheets of paper, and one page of information on average equals 20 kilobytes (.02 megabytes).This page-to-data size conversion factor is conservative. For example, collections consisting largely of e-mails and spreadsheets may have a conversion factor of .01 or even .005, resulting in two to four times as many "pages" or page-equivalents.

The Importance of Chain of Custody

A defensible chain of custody is clearly vital, yet the passage of time can pose some unexpected challenges. Larger legal cases can often last for years, and information technology teams often experience frequent turnover. It is critically important, therefore, to gather the contact information for both the subject of the data collection, as well as the person doing the collecting, at the time of collection.

You may want to utilize serial numbers and asset tags to tie the data collected to a specific machine, which thus ties it to a person. You'll also want to track what external devices are on a custodian's machine to ensure knowledge regarding the machine's external media capacity. For example, documenting that the CD drive is a CD-Read Only device will reduce the likelihood that the opposition can charge that CD backups were produced from that custodian's computer.

This physical audit trail to the electronic data can be of crucial importance. Appendix G of this guide provides sample data collection checklists that are useful for managing the process with appropriate documentation. The primary purpose for this level of detail is that the data collection staff will not have to rely on memory should they need to be deposed. The chain of custody forms can become business records if they are used reliably.

Managing chain of custody includes maintaining physical and/or automated records of chronological and logistical information such as:

▶ What was the source of the data (custodian and location)?

▶ Where on the hard drive were individual files physically located?

▶ Was the collection complete or selective?

▶ Who requested the data and when was the data requested?

▶ When did the data arrive?

▶ What was the complete chain of custody up to the production phase of the project?

See the Appendices for sample forms.

Common Data Collection Questions

Are e-discovery and computer forensics the same thing?

No, e-discovery and computer forensics are not the same thing, but forensics is an important subset of the e-discovery process. e-Discovery focuses on collection of large quantities of data to determine what's relevant while forensics typically focuses on finding specific files or fragments on specific machines. The first requirement for e-discovery is to find and record all necessary "live," or easily accessible, files on a company's network. Digital information, however, is not always readily accessible. Computer forensics allows the collection of deleted, hidden, password-protected and encrypted files, and file fragments.

The discovery of "live data" is essential in almost all cases, where computer forensics is usually required in only limited circumstances, such as cases relating to criminal matters, disgruntled personnel matters, bad faith arguments, intellectual property disputes and/or wrongful termination.

Increasingly, courts are turning to forensics experts to help them when discovery obligations are ignored. Craig Ball, as special master, forensically collected and searched over 5 terabytes of data resulting in case settlement and costs to the party not adhering to their obligations.

To reduce the risk of exposing your work product to the opposition, be certain that your e-discovery partner maintains appropriate confidentiality of information and does not unnecessarily share information with the forensics experts who may be deposed to testifying as to the findings.

What is a program or system file, and why can it be culled?

Program files, like those associated with software applications and operating systems, provide the mechanical ability for items such as documents and spreadsheets to be created and for computers to function. They do not contain any material that the end user has created. Discovery does not need to include these program files, with extensions such as ".EXE," ".HLP," ".DLL," or ".LST," thus they can be culled from the review set via processing the file header. A deeper inquiry may be necessary if your case involves compiled source code.

Your e-discovery vendor should maintain a library to identify and remove common application program files, such as those installed with Microsoft® Office, so that your reviewers will not need to review the standard templates provided with the programs. For example, Microsoft Word comes with many templates and sample files, which on the surface appear to be user-created files due to their file extensions (.dot or .doc). A sophisticated e-discovery partner can cull these templates and samples, thus your review team won't waste time reviewing them. The more sophisticated partner will allow your organization to create their own "exclusion" list based on your custom installations.

How much time will it take to collect?

The amount of time it will take to collect ESI depends on whether it is a forensic or active collection. The number of locations, amount of data, number of drives, type(s) of drives and storage environments (servers, archiving systems, network shares, document management systems, databases, etc) all need to be factored. Forensics collection takes longer than active collection; collecting ESI off servers takes more time than on laptops; and collecting evidence from laptops takes longer than desktops. Other variables include the speed of the network and whether or not the servers are RAID servers. Depending upon the type of matter, number of custodians and volume of data that's been identified as potentially relevant, the collection time required can range from a single day to multiple weeks. Time equates to cost. To quote GE's Senior Counsel for Legal Technology, Jay Brudz, "If it's forensical, it's expensical."

What will custodians' experience be during collection?

This also depends on whether it is a forensics or active collection. Individual custodians may be asked to give up their machines for a short amount of time (1 hour or less for active, 1-3 hours for forensics). In forensics collection, special forensics software will be used and the hard drive quarantined from change so the data can be copied bit by bit. The hard drive from the custodian's computer may be removed and then replaced at the end of the collection. Data can also be collected at night or over the network in some situations.

Why shouldn't attorneys collect the data as they interview witnesses?

Attorneys can assist in collection by identifying the relevant custodians, identifying where the potentially relevant ESI might reside and providing instructions on what's required by the court for documenting protocols. Actually conducting the collection can expose the client or company to legal risks. For example, picking and choosing files by opening them will change the access date and, in the case of Microsoft Office documents, can change the last modified date. Attorneys who pick and choose files can also be called to testify as to the chain of custody of the data they collected and presented to the court. Third-party validation as to the process will be much stronger.

Understand What You Have — Early On

While corporate IT personnel may possess the technical skills required to collect data, they may not have the resources, tools or procedures to analyze, manage and distill the data for the legal process.

An e-discovery partner is helpful at this point, because they can generate basic reports of what has been collected, such as number of files, file types and volume of data. Your collection partner can also create an evidentiary log documenting all processes and procedures conducted during the collection process.

This information will enable you to make informed decisions before processing the data, as well as in the "meet and confer" negotiations, and ensure that the process is defensible. Your e-discovery partner can also help you store the data and images on appropriate media in a secure storage facility, ensuring that it is recoverable over time.

CHAPTER 7

Data Processing: Aggregating for True Visibility

Before processing or handling the files in any way, please refer back to the previous chapter on collection to make an evidence grade copy of your original. Never work on the original evidence, not even to just take a gander at what is in there.

Once data has been collected, you'll need a way to review it in a format that allows full visibility of every responsive aspect. You'll also want the ability to do large-scale data searches of the entire data set, rather than by individual data custodians one at a time.

For this to be done efficiently, the review set must be aggregated into a unified evidence database. To create a comprehensive and secure database of original file content and associated metadata, your best option for defensibly managing the ESI is to convert it into a common, viewable format, such as HTML, TIFF or PDF, while at the same time, maintaining access to the native file.

"Native file" review is becoming a popular concept; however, most, if not all, native file review environments employ viewing technology that will give a snapshot of a file and not necessarily the whole file optimally exposed for review.

The most useful unified databases are fully indexed, designed for large-scale searching and optimized to support a variety of review formats, including the web, electronic or paper.

Data processing should include capturing a digital fingerprint (in techno-speak, a unique "hash" code) of each file for authenticity purposes, documenting the chain of custody. Files should be virus-scanned.

To minimize cost, and when appropriate, ESI should be reduced (also known as evidence screening, culling, pre-culling and pre-searching) before full processing. Data reduction includes winnowing out operating system and program files; identifying and reducing duplicates; and culling based on file type, custodian and date ranges. This reduction can include keyword search terms for culling or simply pre-categorization of potentially privileged evidence or non-responsive documents.

Some platforms encourage reduction based on "conceptual" engines. Be careful here as you may need to explain your reduction protocol and need to say more than "the machine said it was not responsive." Statistical analysis can provide a strong foundation for reduction in this way, as can a "Boolean backup" exercise.

When instructing your partner to reduce data, make sure to have a quality check to make sure it was properly done. One litigant found out the hard way that privilege was lost when their vendor accidentally processed (and produced) e-mails deleted from Lotus Notes intended to be held back for privilege. The reduction (and review) was done natively by the attorneys. They sent the reduced file to a vendor to process and produce after deleting what they thought were the only copies in a privileged folder. Unknown to them, Lotus Notes also has an "All documents" folder. The only thing they accomplished was deleting the privileged designation.[59]

Sedona Principle 10:
A responding party should follow reasonable procedures to protect privileges and objections in connection with the production of electronically stored information.

---

59 Amersham Biosciences Corp. v. PerkinElmer, Inc., 2007 WL 329290 (D.N.J. Jan. 31, 2007 (Unpublished))

Data Culling

What Is Metadata, and Why Is It Important?

Metadata is often described as "data about the data." It includes information, such as file dates, authors, source locations and e-mail routing information, which generally does not appear on the printed page. The e-discovery process offers the best method to preserve and access such metadata, which can contain important information about who created and reviewed electronic documents and to whom they were distributed.

Metadata is indicative of, but not definitive of, dates, creators of documents and other properties. Metadata is collected and stored differently by each application program. Each version of the same program can treat metadata differently. A full-service e-discovery services provider can help you understand the nuances of metadata and ensure that your data is collected, produced and interpreted with impeccable chain of custody procedures. The provider should also be able to export all types of metadata to your review database.

There are data elements or embedded data in files like spreadsheets (formulas) or word processing documents (track changes) which are technically not metadata, but are sometimes treated that way.[60]

There are five key types of metadata your e-discovery partner should identify and manage:

---

60 Williams v. Spring/United Mgmt. Co., 230 F.R.D. 640 (D. Kan. 2005) requiring production with metadata intact (formulas). See succeeding cases regarding privilege, sanctions and productions in more than one form.

▶ File system metadata – data that can be obtained or extracted about a file from the original file system storing the file.

▶ Document metadata – data stored in the document about the document. Often this data is not immediately viewable in the application used to create/edit the document but often can be accessed via a "Properties" view.

▶ E-mail metadata – data stored in the e-mail about the e-mail. Often this data is not even viewable in e-mail client applications used to create the e-mail. The amount of e-mail metadata available for a particular e-mail varies greatly depending on the e-mail system.

▶ Vendor-added metadata – data created and maintained by your e-discovery vendor as a result of processing the item. While some of the vendor-added metadata has direct value to you, much of it is used for process reporting, chain of custody and data accountability.

▶ Client-added metadata – data or "work product" created by a client while reviewing the document set.

Metadata	Description	Type
File Class	Generic class of a document. Examples: "Spreadsheet," "Graphics," "Word Processing"	File System
File Type	File type (or "signature") determined by vendor by analyzing the file (regardless of file extension). Examples: "Microsoft® Excel 2000" or "Word Perfect 5.0"	File System
File Size	File size of the document in bytes.	File System
Date Last Modified	Date and time the file was last saved.	File System
Read Only	Specifies whether a file or folder is read-only, which means that it cannot be changed or accidentally deleted.	File System
Encrypted	Specifies whether a file or folder is encrypted. This is metadata from the file system; not available for e-mails.	File System
Title	Title of the document as entered by the author, or already present in the document template.	Document
Subject	Subject of the document as entered by the author, or already present in the document template.	Document

Author	Author of the document, typically automatically entered by the application by reading the local computer's settings. The actual author of the document can typically overwrite this value.	Document
Manager	Manager of the author of the document as entered by the author, or already present in the document template.	Document
Company	Company of the author of the document as entered by the author, or already present in the document template.	Document
To:	Names of the recipients of an e-mail	E-mail
From:	Name of the sender of the e-mail	E-mail
Date:	Sent, received and modified dates for e-mails	E-mail
BCC	Names of blind carbon-copied recipients of an e-mail.	E-mail
Importance	Importance value assigned to e-mail. Examples: "High," "Normal," and "Low"	E-mail
Metadata	Description	Type
Sender Name	Name of the e-mail sender. This may be a fully qualified e-mail address (ralph.jones@acme.com) or an alias used by the e-mail system (Ralph Jones).	E-mail
Sensitivity	Sensitivity value assigned to e-mail. Examples: "Normal" and "Confidential"	E-mail
Sent On	Date and time the e-mail was sent.	E-mail
Sent On Behalf Of Name	Name of the true sender of the e-mail (whether by proxy or by name that appears in Sender Name).	E-mail
Bates	The Bates range assigned to a document. Because some vendors support producing a document multiple times to multiple parties, a document may have any number of Bates ranges.	Vendor-added
Date Published	Date and time a document, media, shipment or case was published to the data review tool.	Vendor-added
Duplicate Status	A flag used to indicate a document is a dup-duplicate of another document in the data collection. Extremely useful in filtering out duplicates.	Vendor-added
Read/Unread	A flag used to track whether an individual user of the data review tool has read a document.	Vendor-added
Categories	List of the categories associated with a document or e-mail.	Customer-added
Annotation Comment	Free-form text of the annotation added by a customer. A single document can have multiple annotations.	Customer-added
Annotation Selected Text	The section of a document about which the annotation was made.	Customer-added

Again it is important to note if Local Rules clarify definitions around metadata. For instance, Maryland's ESI Protocol[61] describes three types of metadata:

1) **System Metadata:** Data that is automatically generated by a computer system. For example, system metadata includes information such as author, date, and time of creation, and the date a document was modified.

2) **Substantive Metadata:** is data that reflects the substantive changes made to the document by the user. For example, it may include the text of actual changes to a document. While no generalization is universally applicable, system metadata is less likely to involve issues of work product and/or privilege.

3) **Embedded Metadata:** means text, numbers, content, data, or information that is directly or indirectly inputted into a Native File by a user and which is not typically visible to the user viewing the output of display of the Native File on screen or as a print-out.

It is beneficial to have an agreement on production of metadata as an outcome of the meet and confer.

Since it is difficult to forsee when metadata will be important, perhaps for authentication purposes, it is critical to have evidence grade collection to maintain dates. Metadata does not need to be extracted if a clean copy of the native file is available. General practice now is to extract metadata in processing to aid in review and for potential production.

Sophisticated Identification of Duplicates
Just "getting rid of duplicate files" should never be considered as an effective solution. You need to make sure there is a legally defensible audit trail for any duplicate files before you delete them. The question of who had access to what and when is often very relevant and can be missed if duplicate data files are automatically deleted. Experienced litigation support managers recognize the value of identifying duplicates across the whole data set so that the "dupes" can be coded and categorized consistently. This

---

61 http://www.mdd.uscourts.gov/news/news/ESIProtocol.pdf

will reduce the time and effort expended by your data review team and, at the same time, allows flexibility for productions in a different order than the initial loading of files.

Take care with near dup technology. Make sure it is paired with a protocol to protect privilege. Going too wide with near dup reduction can eliminate the privileged documents and leave non-privileged files. Or it may eliminate non-privileged, responsive documents, putting your entire privilege log into play during an in camera challenge.

Pitfalls with E-mail Culling

An overly aggressive, unconditional de-duplication strategy with document sets containing e-mail can lead to undesirable results and significant legal liabilities (e.g. spoliation or evidence tampering claims). Some e-discovery vendors new to the field practice such a strategy because it results in short-term cost reduction. Yes, there will be fewer documents to review – only one copy of any given item within the entire document set. However, this kind of de-duplication doesn't allow you to see the ESI in, or produce it from, the other locations or contexts in which it originally resided. The broader context of a document – who had access to it, whether it can be determined to be "unread," and to which e-mails it was attached – is often critical to the issues of a matter (see Tips on e-mail chains and threads and why they matter).

A more sophisticated approach to culling is to flag or track each instance of a document where it exists in a unique context. e-Discovery professionals often describe the different contexts in terms of different document "chains."

For example, consider the case in which Ms. A created a word-processed memo and saved it to her computer's hard drive in her "memos" folder. Ms. A then sent the e-mail to her boss, explaining the legal risks of the attached memo. Later, Ms. A sent another e-mail to a number of people on the management team of her company, again attaching the same memo but this time without any legal risk caveats.

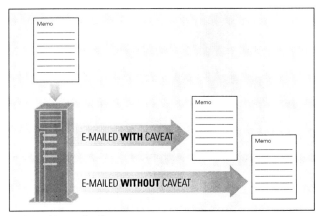

Pitfalls with e-mail culilng.

A more junior, less-experienced e-discovery partner might decide that all three instances of the memo are "equal" duplicates and thus provide only the first (or third) instance to the discovery team to review. The critical second instance, demonstrating awareness of legal risks, is then missed. The liability of this approach is compounded should the discovery team later "re-duplicate" the document set at production time.

The fundamental flaw is failing to consider the various contexts in which the memo existed. A sophisticated e-discovery partner will recognize the three instances of the memo itself as duplicates but will flag them such that the discovery team reviews each instance within the three very different contexts – only one of which demonstrates the author's (highly relevant) knowledge of the legal risk of the memo.

TIP: The Difference Between Chains and Threads

An e-mail "chain" is the e-mail plus its attachments, including files, other e-mails with their attachments (nest attachments), and embedded links to other documents or web pages.

An e-mail "thread" is the history and the progression of an e-mail topic, including the various replies, forwards and added recipients.

Duplicate Identification Methods

There are five primary methods for identification of duplicates: Backup, Across Case and Within Custodian, near dup and production de-duplication. The preference is a legal decision. The differences between the three methods are as follows:

Backup de-duplication looks for and retains single copies of documents in the exact same context. If an identical document name, path, date and file size is found on 10 backup tapes, it can be assumed that it is the same file and only one copy of the file needs to be preserved. Unless there is bad faith alleged, it is unlikely that you will need to report on each file of the backup tape.

Across Case de-duplication looks for and retains single copies of documents per case. So, if an identical document resides with Mr. A, Mr. B and Mr. C, only the first occurrence of the file (i.e., Mr. A's) will be saved.

Within Custodian de-duplication only de-duplicates a document if multiple copies of that document reside within the same custodian's data set. So if Mr. A and Mr. B each have a copy of a specific document, and Mr. C has two copies, the system will maintain one copy each for Mr. A, Mr. B and Mr. C.

Near dup de-duplication will de-duplicate drafts, and other files that are almost the same. If you had a document and inserted the word "not" into it, the two documents would be near dups. Identifying near dups is extremely helpful to speed review but is not a panacea to reduce the need to look at key documents.

When it comes time to produce, some partners provide another very useful method for de-duplicating: production.

Production de-duplication. Like custodian de-duplication, production de-duplication only de-duplicates a document if multiple copies of that document reside within the same production set. So, if two identical documents are both marked responsive, non-privileged, the system will only produce one of those documents.

Another pitfall of poorly considered de-duplication is that you may end up producing incomplete e-mail chains in which attachments have been lost. For example, you want to avoid the situation where the same file is attached to two different e-mails, both marked responsive, yet one of the attachments is not produced because it is automatically screened out as "duplicate." This would result in a broken or incomplete chain that might indicate that the attachment is missing and raise questions. Ask your partner if they support a rule that ensures that a chain of e-mails and attachments are always produced together, trumping all other de-duplication rules.

Some e-discovery partners or software packages can only thoroughly de-duplicate e-mails but not stand-alone files, such as word processing documents or spreadsheets. Others are able to do precise file comparisons to identify unique or identical files. You'll want to be sure that your e-discovery partner can do precise file comparisons for all types of files, not just e-mail.

Not all e-discovery partners or software packages can recognize and natively process e-mail that is stored in other formats, like Eudora, Unix- or Linux-based mail or GroupWise. Some systems will convert even the popular Lotus Notes. Almost all process Microsoft® Outlook (Exchange) e-mail natively, although newer products may have trouble with earlier versions of Outlook. If there is conversion, generally to .PST, make sure your legal team understands what is lost, such as some dates or special metadata.

E-mail archiving is growing in popularity and is used for preservation. The caution here is that many systems do not have the capability to retain the original context (foldering) associated with the e-mails and may only keep one copy of an e-mail, pointing to it from other mail boxes. Many systems can extract and produce one or two e-mails at a time without issue, but they may not be able to efficiently support production when a massive export is required. It's important to know the capabilities and limitations of your e-mail archiving system, so you can include it into your whole infrastructure view for e-discovery — before you need it. It is also critical to understand what the archive system considers a "duplicate."

TIP: The Importance of E-Mail Chains

To get full visibility into your data, you'll need access to complete e-mail chains, including the original e-mail and all of its attachments. This is critically important because you often need to produce the entire chain and, therefore, need to review a chain in its entirety to determine if any single item is confidential or privileged.

Thorough Data Processing

Data processing for e-discovery requires expertise in various technologies. Electronic document populations generally contain large volumes of disparate file types. For an e-discovery project to be successful, this data must be processed and aggregated quickly and reliably.

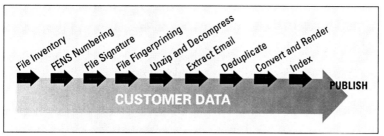

Data processing.

Your e-discovery partner should be able to help you:

▶ Fully inventory and uniquely number each file in the data population for file accountability. Normally, this involves digital fingerprinting (or "hashing") each file for authenticity and chain of custody.

▶ Maintain a log of all passwords required to access files. Without this log, it will be difficult to secure prompt access to important file information. Make sure that your partner can break the passwords for critical data custodians. For ultra-secure platforms, such as Lotus Notes, make sure your partner knows the requests to make of the administrators.

▶ Uncompress files while maintaining the folder structure of the compressed files. Also, decompression must be done recursively, so that if you have a parent ZIP file that contains a set of children ZIP files, all files will be uncompressed and ready for review, not just the parent ZIP file.

▶ Digitally identify each file's signature to determine its true file type rather than relying on the file's extension, which is often inaccurate.

▶ Remove operating system and program (software application) files based on a defensible process, such as the National Institute of Standards and Technology (NIST) list used by forensic experts and law enforcement.

▶ Cull your data based on file type, custodian, date ranges and/or pre-determined search terms.

▶ Flag duplicate files, so they may be filtered out during later stages. You should be able to produce all original native files, including duplicates you may have filtered.

▶ Extract file content and metadata from the files, such as e-mail routing data, file property data and other "hidden" data that can be relevant during discovery.

▶ Convert the desired electronic documents to common viewable format. Ideally, you should convert to a higher fidelity, more interactive format like HTML rather than a static format, such as TIFF or PDF. This often is most cost-effective and enables reviewers to hit-highlight, copy text to the clipboard, and select text or mark annotations. Since HTML is not a paginated format like TIFF or PDF, it provides a far more efficient way to review complex documents like spreadsheets.

At this stage, you have the option of merging your electronic documents with paper documents that have been scanned and/or optically character recognized (OCRed).

Preparing E-mail

Most often, e-mail messages and attachments are stored in the form of self-contained mailbox files that reside on network servers. E-mails may also reside on the data custodian's desktop computer, either manually saved to a hard drive by the user or automatically moved from the active inbox to the hard drive for archiving purposes via rules and e-mail handling settings. Difficulties can arise if mailbox files are collected and reviewed incorrectly. For example, if an attorney reviews files from within an e-mail software program, critical content and metadata may change automatically as each file is opened and read, or if it is forwarded or copied. Further, if the mailbox contained unsent messages in the "Outbox," an attorney opening the mailbox may inadvertently send the outbound messages automatically. Upon exit, an automatic "empty recycle bin" rule may be invoked.

If your client has a significant amount of electronic communication, you have to open each custodian's e-mail message box one at a time. If you're opening messages from within the e-mail software application, you may not be able to do global searches on the attachments associated with the messages. Although you can search the e-mail message content, the attachments provide valuable information that you'll need to access for full data review. Not searching attachments was one of the discovery failings noted by the judge in the Morgan Stanley case.[62]

Efficiency in review is also difficult due to the sheer volume of e-mail communications in today's workplace. About 171 billion e-mails are sent daily[63] and the usage of instant messaging (IM) is increasing. According to The Radicati Group, the number of worldwide IM accounts will grow from 995 million in 2006 to over 1.6 billion by 2010. These percentages can only be expected to rise. Moreover, the increasing use of Voice over IP (VoIP), which uses the Internet for telephone communication and then stores voice mails on servers similar to conventional e-mail, adds another source of ESI to consider. These audio and voice mail files are often subject to discovery during an SEC investigation.

Limitations of Litigation Support Packages
Early litigation support software packages were primarily designed to accommodate scans of paper documents. They have subsequently been upgraded to support TIFF images of electronic documents. Some litigation support packages indicate that they manage electronic documents via tagging and searching the information, but they may not provide sufficient functionality for a defensible review.

To avoid this logistical hassle, you should consider using technology that will allow you to convert native files into TIFF files so you can Bates-stamp the images and automatically track them.

Some electronic litigation support packages can process e-mail but can't create TIFF images of the review set. After legal teams complete the review, they may not be able to accurately or efficiently output the results and reliably track production.

TIP: Taking Out the Garbage
You may find that your client provides a massive amount of data, yet much of it serves no purpose, such as system and software application files that do not contain relevant content. You can save significant amounts of time by having your client's files cataloged, so unneeded files can be quickly filtered out. Well-structured, efficient pre-culling and categorization of ESI via search terms are highly recommended methods prior to creating the data review/control set.

---

62 See Coleman (Parent) Holdings, Inc. vs. Morgan Stanley & Co., Inc., 2005 WL 679071 (Fla. Cir. Ct. Mar. 1, 2005)

63 March 2006 report from The Radicati Group, a market research company

Sedona Principle 12:

Absent party agreement or court order specifying the form or forms of production, production should be made in the form or forms in which the information is ordinarily maintained or in a reasonably usable form, taking into account the need to produce reasonably accessible metadata that will enable the receiving party to have the same ability to access, search, and display the information as the producing party where appropriate or necessary in light of the nature of the information and the needs of the case.

Time Zone Challenges

When preparing data, your e-discovery partner must be able to manage date and time complexities. You may need to combine e-mails from various offices throughout the nation or the world. This introduces time zone issues, even as common as East Coast vs. West Coast or daylight vs. standard time. Date/time sequences can be crucial in identifying who knew what when, yet the sequences will be incorrect unless you base it all on a standard, such as Greenwich Mean Time (GMT). As an added complexity, Windows® 95 stores dates differently than Windows® 2000. Fortunately, all of these date and time issues can be handled by an experienced e-discovery partner.

International Data

If you have international data, particularly picture-based languages, make sure your provider can handle what is called Unicode data. Unicode is used to ensure an accurate graphic representation of what is sometimes called double byte data. Alphanumeric, romance language characters can be represented by one byte in computer language. Picture-based languages, like Mandarin, require two bytes for an accurate representation.

Once your data is properly converted into a unified evidence database and published to a common repository, you are ready to begin the fourth and often most time consuming step of a discovery project – document review.

CHAPTER 8

Data Review: Fast and Thorough Methods

During the discovery phase of large or complex cases, there can be significant time and resource burdens associated with document review. Reviewing printed versions of electronic materials can be a time-consuming process. It is also subject to risks of omission due to "reviewer's fatigue," resulting in potential misidentification and misclassification of relevant and privileged evidence.

To reduce fatigue and meet tight e-discovery response deadlines imposed by courts and government agencies, legal teams should use reliable electronic data review tools that are fast and efficient. Pick the vendor or products that enable this. The review platform must scale to meet the demands of a project of any size, support review teams dispersed in multiple locations, and provide a means for tracking progress to ensure that all ESI is reviewed thoroughly and accurately.

Have in place a protocol that maps technology and techniques to the review goals. You may want to create "if yes/if no" decision trees, along with category or issue coding lists to help guide review. Avoid the natural tendency to treat electronic documents just like paper documents. For example, a traditional approach to a paper review is to code documents by type, such as memos, letters, spreadsheets, notices, presentations or meeting agendas/

minutes. Most e-discovery partners will identify document types automatically via a reliable, repeatable signature process, which is not subject to the natural variances of coding done by humans. Admittedly, these automated processes do not differentiate meeting minutes from memos. Instead, they identify them both as word processed documents. Yet at the end of the day, the task is to make a quick, sound judgment as to the document's relevancy or confidentiality/privilege status. Any further coding is often a waste of time given the benefits of accurate full-text searching.

Sedona Principle 11:

A responding party may satisfy its good faith obligation to preserve and produce relevant electronically stored information by using electronic tools and processes, such as data sampling, searching, or the use of selection criteria, to identify data reasonably likely to contain relevant information.

TIP: What You Don't See on Paper

When electronic information is directly converted to paper for review, information, such as metadata, linkages between e-mail messages and attachments, hidden or changed text in word processing documents, formulas and hidden rows and columns in spreadsheets can be lost and, therefore, never seen. You'll want to utilize the appropriate e-discovery tools and processes to ensure this doesn't happen.

This chapter covers some general tips and important considerations when establishing review strategies and assumes that ESI will be hosted by an experienced, third-party provider.

Sedona Principle 13:

Absent a specific objection, party agreement or court order, the reasonable costs of retrieving and reviewing electronically stored information should be borne by the responding party, unless the information sought is not reasonably available to the responding party in the ordinary course of business. If the information sought is not reasonably available to the responding party in the ordinary course of business, then, absent special circumstances, the costs of retrieving and reviewing such electronic information may be shared by or shifted to the requesting party.

Safeguard the Data

Once the data has been gathered and aggregated, it needs to be safeguarded so you can confidently and securely review it. Make sure the review system is redundant and protected. If your e-discovery partner is hosting the ESI, make sure the provider utilizes the latest in data center security technologies and the best practices in deploying, handling and protecting assets and your information.

The data center should be physically secured, such as accessible by a two factor authentication system, and electronically secure. Protections should include utilizing state-of-the-art, double-firewall systems to fully isolate the hosted data and encrypt SSL connections. Other standard protections include a robust intrusion detection system. E-mail correspondence with your e-discovery partner may need to be conducted using 512-bit encryption and digital certificates. Post-litigation protections should include wipes of the project data and/or return of your materials.

Ways to Reduce Search and Review Time

There is a misperception about e-discovery that you'll have to read thousands of documents online. In reality, the sophisticated search capabilities available in today's e-discovery data review tools can reduce the document count dramatically. For example, it's common to collect 100 gigabytes, cull the system files, and de-duplicate the evidence set, resulting in the legal team only being required to physically review less than 10 gigabytes of potentially relevant evidence.

For the most accurate and efficient data review process, utilizing a web-based (online) review tool will enable your legal team to search, organize, categorize, annotate, cull and produce information. The goal is to minimize the time and resources you need to allocate to the search and review process while protecting the integrity of the data. Online discovery enables remote, secure access to your data for concurrent review by members of your team, regardless of location.

Combine Electronic and Hard Copy

You'll want the ability to import hard copy images and associated text into your data review set, so you can review them concurrently with the electronic documents. Make sure your review provider can create and control a master data repository containing both paper-based imaged documents and electronic documents. Usually, this means you'll want them to have the hard copy documents converted to TIFF images, preserving all associated page-level text, Bates numbers, and document groupings based upon your specifications.

E-mail Chains

There is often more to an e-mail than the distribution list, subject line and body. E-mail messages are complex items with "chains," such as any number of attachments and nested attachments or e-mails attached to e-mails attached to e-mails. To expedite a review, you want a tool that displays or maps the complete chain and allows you to quickly and directly navigate to any item in the chain. Sophisticated tools should be able to clearly display the chain's custodian and provide basic information about each item, such as its file type, ID number, the number of "descendent" items beneath each branch of the chain, and each item's coding or category information. It is important to note the flexibility in coding: the whole chain, item by item, or from a particular item downward. Reviews can be constrained if coding can only be applied to the whole e-mail or if a review team must review each and every item of a chain.

Concept Searching

Being able to find, review and produce electronic documents that are conceptually related to initial search queries allows legal teams to identify and review relevant documents more quickly and more accurately than traditional search tools. Unlike keyword searching, which requires skillful use of Boolean operators like "AND" and "OR," concept searching has no required formatting or syntax. Reviewers can enter a natural language query or paste entire paragraphs from a relevant document and, within seconds, receive a list of all related documents ranked by relevancy. Conceptual searching often helps a review team understand the nature or themes of their document set quickly, aids in the review prioritization of different segments of the document set, and helps reviewers form better, more comprehensive keyword searches. Many teams use conceptual searching to speed assignment of potentially hot and privileged documents to the higher-priced attorneys and allocate other less important, but still reviewable, documents offshore or to a contract review facility. There are some new technologies that allow visualization of communication patterns or concepts that can be brought to bear defensibly augmented by a strong validation protocol.

Review Efficiency

When establishing review strategies and the technology needed to support the process, it's important to look at system efficiency in order to accurately predict the speed of your review. This becomes especially important when attempting to extrapolate the total cost of a document review for use in early "meet and confer" negotiations around undue burden and cost shifting.

Here are a few points to keep in mind when establishing an efficient review process:

▶ **Flexible platform.** The most important way to minimize the cost of a discovery project is to use efficient tools that are flexible enough to fit your review team's workflow. Compare the ways different applications support common tasks, such as searching, categorizing and browsing. For example, while the time to actually run a search is important, you also need to consider the time it takes to define the search and review the results. How flexible is the search user interface? How many criteria can be combined? How easy is it to add and remove search criteria? How easy is it to save a search and pull up a saved search? Can saved searches be shared across the review team?

▶ **Individual vs. family.** Consider how well the application in question supports efficient review of complex e-mail families or chains. Does the application support categorizing or tagging an entire chain at once?

▶ **Mouse clicks and shortcuts.** If you really want to compare application efficiency rather than performance (single dimension), start counting mouse clicks and key presses. Less is more. Make sure your review tool can be "driven" by a keyboard as well as a mouse, as keyboard input is roughly three times faster than a mouse.[64]

---

64 Study conducted by F1-Key LLC (www.f1key.com)

Review for Privilege and Relevance

Create a list of all counsel and law firm names ahead of time, so that potentially privileged items can be separated from the evidence set at the beginning of the review cycle. This will help your team eliminate the "bad" review calls, provide greater protection during review, and deliver a more complete production set – faster and more efficiently.

Step One: Define the Criteria for Relevance and Privilege

While this may seem like an obvious step, establishing the criteria for categorizing documents as potentially relevant or privileged can have a profound impact on the effectiveness of the data review. The larger the number of reviewers on your project, the more important it becomes to clearly document criteria for categorizations. Any ambiguities in the criteria will prolong the review and may delay the project.

Step Two: Review for Relevance

▶ Conduct a first-pass review of the documents for relevance, and flag the questionable documents. There is an emerging trend for machine aided, offshore or contract review for the first pass review to reduce costs.

▶ Conduct a second-pass review of the subset of documents that have been marked as potentially relevant. Optionally, do a statistical review of the documents marked "not relevant" for defensibility.

Step Three: Review for Privilege

▶ Use your review platform to create a privilege log. Sophisticated review tools automatically track privileged information and allow you to generate a privilege log at the end of your review.

▶ Search your relevant documents for privilege with firm names, attorney names and other indications of privilege. Your e-discovery vendor will be able to help you construct a search. Conduct a first-pass review of documents for privilege. Flag privileged documents and record the privilege claim. Flag partially privileged documents to be redacted later.

▶ Conduct a second-pass review of documents for privilege, fine tuning the privilege log. Use the platform to create much of the log by generating to author, recipients, dates, pages and general privilege categories. Augment where appropriate to include supporting data increasingly called for to maintain the privilege. (Example: e-mail requesting legal advice to support designation of attorney client communication.)

▶ Redact documents that are partially privileged, and include that data in the privilege log.

Proper Indexing Is Crucial

A common problem in data review, as well as during data processing, is a lack of completely indexed data. The quality of the indexing is very important, as it is the key to finding the data you need. A variety of indexing methods is available; your choice will depend on the nature of your data.

For e-mail, it is best to extract all the e-mail metadata, including the body of the e-mail and attachments, and then build an index for searching. In their original form, e-mail messages and their attachments are contained in a single large "mailbox" file. For example, Microsoft® Exchange mail systems typically store e-mails in a ".PST" file, while Lotus Notes® mail systems usually store e-mails in an ".NSF" file. If you were to do a keyword search on a mailbox file, you may not be able to search the individual e-mail and attachments within either file.

Once all the content is extracted from a mailbox, however, each individual e-mail message, all its metadata and any attachments are available for searching. For example, you can then pull up only those documents that were sent or received by a particular person. There are some intriguing desktop search tools emerging in the marketplace, yet none of them have a defensible way to extract the e-mails without changing critical data and have disclaimers about being used "as forensics tools." Check discoveryresources.org for news on such tools. For all other files, it is best to do native file indexing because those files do not have the same limitations that affect e-mail files.

It's also important to make sure your e-discovery partner has quality control processes in place to track exception files – those files that were not able to be indexed and not available through a database search but still may be critical to a case.

The Right Search Terms

One pitfall in the review stage is the use of overly broad search terms, such as "office," "company name," or "contract." This can result in a massive number of irrelevant hits. You need to ensure that your search parameters and mechanisms appropriately narrow the resulting data set. You'll want to be able to do things like proximity searches. This includes looking for the word "contract" within a number of words or another word, such as "contract w/5 of employment." You'll also want to utilize your review tool's search engine to do specific sub-searches within metadata fields, such as "to," "from" and "subject."

Using e-discovery data review tools efficiently will enable searches to be done on an impressive number of terms. Advanced tools can do simultaneous searches in excess of 2,500 characters. Depending on word count, that can average between 300 and 500 words during a single search. Make sure that your search tool allows you to exclude certain sets of data from your search. This is critical when your data is flowing into the system at different times.

Data File Extensions – There's More Than Meets the Eye

Unless you're using appropriate search technology, data file extensions can be problematic during review. As an example, the file extension for a Microsoft® Word document, which is traditionally .doc, can be changed to other file extensions, such as, exe, .psd and .xls. It is very simple for a data custodian to alter file extensions within his or her data set. Some programs even change file extensions on their own. For instance, when "auto-saving" documents, some word processing programs save temporary or hidden ".TMP" files. While much of this can be addressed with your discovery partner during the processing phase, it's important to understand these file systems during review as well.

Consider the scenario where Mr. Smith altered the file extensions on a set of confidential documents. Later, the data reviewer who gathered Mr. Smith's computer files and searched the entire data set for "*.doc," which was supposed to turn up all word processing documents, would not find all the requested files. The benefit of using sophisticated data review tools that utilize sophisticated search technology is that they will search through all content, thus eliminating the risk of missing critical evidence.

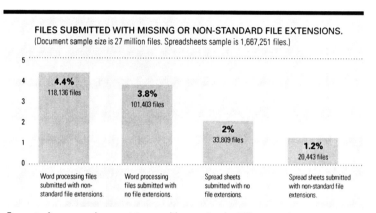

FILES SUBMITTED WITH MISSING OR NON-STANDARD FILE EXTENSIONS.
(Document sample size is 27 million files. Spreadsheets sample is 1,667,251 files.)

Percent of common document types with non-standard file extensions.

Time Crunch

Despite the best intentions, litigation teams don't always allow enough time during the planning process for data review, which can cause a problematic time crunch. If you are in a situation where you need to quickly assign additional document reviewers to your project, you'll want to be sure your vendor doesn't charge you on a per-seat license basis, causing your costs to go up. Potentially more detrimental than the extra seat fees could be the delays in purchasing the licenses, setting up the new accounts or installing new software.

Some law firms use data review tools that are provided on a per-seat basis and share individual passwords among multiple data reviewers. Aside from potentially violating software license agreements, such activity results in reduced security and data reliability. You should be able to authenticate exactly who had access to confidential client data and who reviewed each document. Every system user should be accessing the data set via his or her unique account and password.

The Dark Side of Unprotected Desk-side Data Review

When a company provides data or access to custodian desktops to its law firm, attorneys or in-house litigation support staff may be tempted to do a desk-side, native file review. This involves opening and identifying which files meet the relevance criteria and then copying the files over to another location. The risks of doing an unprotected review of data are significant:

▶ It increases the risk of infecting files with viruses.

▶ Opening and/or moving files that have auto-date or auto-path features activated can change dates and file path references associated with the file, even though you didn't intentionally modify the content. This is where modern applications with default "AutoSave" features can get you into big trouble.

▶ Drag and drop activity with files can also automatically change file reference dates, such as the Create date. If your legal proceeding is date sensitive, you can inadvertently cause the data to be included or excluded from the "response set."

▶ Modern e-mail systems are often configured to automatically send e-mail stored in the "outbox" every few minutes. Depending on the state of the mailbox when the custodian last accessed it, this auto-send feature can cause inadvertent transmission of e-mails by the reviewer.

▶ Legal teams can encounter unwanted liability if their desktop reviews result in an alteration, damage or total erasure of an important piece of evidence.

After your litigation team has performed a detailed review of the data, you'll be ready for the fifth and final step of a discovery project – producing document sets to the requesting parties.

Track Changes in Office Documents, Is that a draft?

At the beginning of the review, review managers need to decide how to handle track changes in Microsoft Word. If documents contain track changes, those could be considered draft documentation and potentially protected under attorney privileges. You should work with your partner and counsel in order to determine the best review and production strategy for these types of documents.

CHAPTER 9

Data Production: Speed, Flexibility and Accuracy

Once your team has reviewed all documents associated with the discovery process, the relevant, non-privileged data set must be delivered to parties such as opposing counsel, partner firms, outside counsel or the requesting government agency. It's important to remember that the format of production, under the FRCP amendments, can be dictated by the requesting party, where the producing party must comply or persuade that another method is better.[65] In addition to understanding what formats your organization can best support in advance of the Rule 26(f) "meet and confer" discovery conferences, you'll want to be sure that your e-discovery vendor can produce ESI in a variety of delivery formats, including TIFFs or PDFs for viewing in Web repositories, third-party case management tools or other databases, native files and paper.

Gap-free Bates Production

It is common for files to require some level of manual intervention for successful processing. Files that are encrypted, password-protected and/or those containing macros need special attention to make them print-ready. The challenge during production is that

---

65 FRCP Rule 34(b)

you'll want all of the documents produced in a specific order to maintain an appropriate Bates numbering sequence. Therefore, rather than printing directly from a file, it is best to convert the file into a page based format like the TIFF format and then print it. Any problematic files will be discovered during the TIFF creation stage and can be addressed prior to printing. This prevents confusion, eliminates labor-intensive assembly and assures consistent, gap-free Bates numbering.

Readability and Fonts

Having the appropriate fonts loaded into the production system is vital to properly rendering and producing the wide variety of files generally found in electronic data sets. Documents are often created using a surprising number of standard and nonstandard fonts. If a font is not available, font substitution occurs that can result in visual distortion, such as overlays and other alterations. You'll want to be sure that all fonts are available so documents can be produced in the original format used by the data custodian.

TIP: Data Production Complexities

Your e-discovery service provider can help you identify which types of files are likely to "fail" during the production step. Complications, such as password production, macros or presentations files that are too large, can cause production limitations. You'll want to make sure that your service provider can handle the file complexities, will provide detailed exception reporting for file output and, if necessary, can export native files for review and production.

Multiple Production Options

A crucial aspect of production is accurately and reliably tracking document productions so you know what documents went to which recipients on specific dates. All production information should be tracked within the provider's database. Your providers should also provide you with the option of producing the same documents to multiple recipients, with separate tracking numbers for each, and, if desired, with different Bates numbers. Make sure your provider allows you to search for a document based on a Bates number, so if you are presented with an individual page at deposition time, you can retrieve the entire document to view the page in context and make sure it is what you produced. This will allow good faith productions for matters requiring the same documents. Repositories are being formalized by many serial litigants, saving review time and reducing the risk of inconsistent productions.

TIP: Bates Numbering Capabilities

In anticipation of discovery, you'll want to have a clear understanding of your e-discovery partner's capabilities and limitations with respect to Bates numbering. Be sure the vendor is able to assign multiple Bates numbers to an electronic document in case you'll need to produce it in multiple matters or to multiple recipients. This will enable the reuse of information that has already been reviewed for privilege and relevancy and will save you time in the review stage. You'll also want to know the legal matter for which it was reviewed and the production sets in which it was included.

Problems with Do-it-yourself Production

What you print does not always capture everything in a computer file. Often when producing spreadsheets, the selected print area within a document does not contain all the content of the file. Be sure that any hidden rows, columns and worksheets are unhidden. Spreadsheets also pose the problem of cell contents that are too large for the column or row, resulting in truncated text or placeholder content for numerical data that appears as "######." To prevent this, make sure to re-size the cells so all the content is visible. Your e-discovery vendor should offer the option of performing automatic electronic formatting to reveal such content in spreadsheets. After all the content has been made visible, it is then appropriate to convert the file to HTML, TIFF or PDF.

Producing the Right Documents

You don't want to inadvertently produce privileged or irrelevant documents to the opposition. Mishaps at this stage can be devastating to your case. Be certain that your provider has strict quality control methods in place for document production, as well as be able to provide training to your review team to ensure proper protocols and methodologies are in place in advance of production. Production project managers should clearly understand the data review plan and the methods for data production prior to discovery commencing. This preparation process will help ensure that your data production is fast, clean and accurate. Proposed Federal Rule of Evidence (FRE) 502 is designed to allow clawbacks of inadvertently produced material. It is to be used in combination with the protocol envisioned by FRCP 26(b)(5)(B) to notify, sequester and return privileged material. These are new provisions and many litigation support departments are not prepared to take advantage of these. In addition, FRE 502 will allow unprecedented privilege protection, even as to other parties and cases, if the protocol is blessed by a judge in a formal order rather than an agreement. While FRE 502 is not yet law, if it becomes law, it will take effect upon cases in process, much like the amendments to the FRCP did in 2006.

Depending on the review protocol, there may be some "dup syncing" to do. Be careful that your dup syncing does not undo the good work your review team did. For example, during rolling productions, be wary of protocols that designate individual items in an e-mail chain as privileged rather than at the chain level and then apply that privileged designation to the other duplicates. Imagine the next production when an attachment, privileged only by association with another privileged document, is allowed to control another non-privileged e-mail chain. This will cause an in camera nightmare should your designations be challenged. Privilege challenges are always a popular activity during litigation and will become more popular as the privilege designation gets more important.

Native File Productions

Certain segments of the government and plaintiff's attorneys are leading the charge for native file productions. Many argue that viewing a document in its native format, for example a Word document read in Microsoft® Word, is as close as we can come to seeing and understanding the author's intentions and meanings. There before us lies the formatting, the fonts, the punctuation, the pagination – everything that the writer created (or everything that the last person who touched the document changed or modified). Another argument for native review is that it saves money because the documents in a collection do not need to be processed or converted to .TIFF, HTML or PDF files.

However, reviewing native files by using the corresponding native applications is often a recipe for disaster. Native file review is inherently limited in its ability to find specific documents and often results in logistical nightmares, especially for large, geographically dispersed review teams. Some of the pitfalls you might encounter in native file review include:

▶ Unintentionally altering metadata as files are moved, opened, or reviewed.

▶ The inability to conduct complex keyword searches, depending upon the application.

▶ Insuring that reviewers understand how to exploit the relevant features of the native applications.

▶ The difficulty (or impossibility) of redacting and/or annotating native files.

▶ The difficulty of Bates numbering on a per page basis and the attendant need to create Bates "names" at the file level.

▶ The need to have licensed versions of the applications corresponding to the entire native file types in the review.

There are e-discovery vendors that do offer "pure" native review. Pure native review is accomplished by:

▶ Having reviewers access a central server containing the Microsoft Office applications, the Adobe, Graphics viewers, Visio etc to display the documents.

▶ Having a copy of the above files for each reviewer or

▶ Having a third-party viewer on the desktop of each individual.

The file must be loaded into memory. Where the original application is opening the file, reviewers can widen and unhide columns, look for comments and search hits via a find command. When using a third-party viewer, reviewers are limited to one view, unless the original native file is available for download.

The challenge with native file review is that you have little or no ability to keep track of who has reviewed the document and when that review was complete. Records of this type of handling must be kept to insure that all documents that are to be reviewed actually get reviewed and by the correct reviewer.

So why bother?

The simplest answer is that it may be required by opposition, the courts or regulators. In that case, review in the native format may not be necessary but final production certainly will. Reviewers may wish to see documents exactly as their opposition will see them, a reasonable argument for native review.

Prior to agreeing to a native file production at the initial "meet and confer," understand that the requesting party will have access to the original file, with the hidden columns, tracked changes, comments and versioning history. Requests for native file productions (and the metadata contained therein) are not automatically granted. Generally, a showing must be made why the metadata, like track changes, is responsive. Current practice is that metadata must be preserved, but it may not need to be produced. Spreadsheet formulas are an exception and are generally produced natively.

Most e-discovery partners, regardless of review method, can provide you with a hard drive containing only the responsive, non-privileged native files as part of their normal export process.

Some government agencies are encouraging the use of electronic vaults where they can search and review material without incurring the cost of processing it.

CHAPTER 10

Closing the Loop

The document productions are complete and discovery is over — for this matter.

It is now time to make sure that all produced material (native or page) gets loaded back into your evidence repository. Make sure that multiple productions get loaded so that the different Bates numbers and markings are captured. Make sure the dates of production are noted in the evidence system, or in another system, with the details of the court, date of production, and matter name for easier productions in future litigations or investigations. Many a time, good faith is established by producing material that has been reviewed and produced in previous litigation while the new ESI is being collected and reviewed.

In addition, before jumping into your next challenge, take a little time to ask yourself and your discovery team a few questions. The answers to these questions just might help you save time and money the next time around.

▶ Did you meet your discovery objectives?

▶ Was there a favorable outcome to the case?

▶ Did you have an e-discovery plan ready in advance of the case?

▶ Was your e-discovery plan defensible?

▶ Were your time expectations met?

▶ Were your time expectations reasonable?

▶ Did you have the right team players?

▶ Was order brought to the chaos of the data needed for review?

▶ Did the productions go smoothly?

▶ Did you reduce the cost of review?

▶ Did you reduce the risk of sanctions or malpractice for outside counsel?

▶ Where can process improvements be achieved on future matters?

It's 4:45 p.m., and the project team is celebrating the successful settlement of a two-year investigation. War stories abound. Heroes are feted and the goats of the project are pilloried. The lead attorney gets up to leave, talking about an early family dinner and seeing his children before bed time.

His cell phone rings. It's the lead partner on the case. And no, he's not calling with congratulations. A civil suit has been filed, asking for documents from your investigation…

APPENDIX A

The Sedona Conference Principles
Second Edition, July 2007

The Sedona Principles for Electronic Document Production are as follows:

1. Electronically stored information is potentially discoverable under Fed. R. Civ. P. 34 or its state equivalents. Organizations must properly preserve electronically stored information that can reasonably be anticipated to be relevant to litigation.

2. When balancing the cost, burden, and need for electronically stored information, courts and parties should apply the proportionality standard embodied in Fed. R. Civ. P. 26(b)(2)(C) and its state equivalents, which require consideration of the technological feasibility and realistic costs of preserving, retrieving, reviewing, and producing electronically stored information, as well as the nature of the litigation and the amount in controversy.

3. Parties should confer early in discovery regarding the preservation and production of electronically stored information when these matters are at issue in the litigation and seek to agree on the scope of each party's rights and responsibilities.

4. Discovery requests for electronically stored information should be as clear as possible, while responses and objections to discovery should disclose the scope and limits of the production.

5. The obligation to preserve electronically stored information requires reasonable and good faith efforts to retain information that may be relevant to pending or threatened litigation. However, it is unreasonable to expect parties to take every conceivable step to preserve all potentially relevant electronically stored information.

6. Responding parties are best situated to evaluate the procedures, methodologies, and technologies appropriate for preserving and producing their own electronically stored information.

7. The requesting party has the burden on a motion to compel to show that the responding party's steps to preserve and produce relevant electronically stored information were inadequate.

8. The primary source of electronically stored information for production should be active data and information. Resort to disaster recovery backup tapes and other sources of electronically stored information that are not reasonably accessible requires the requesting party to demonstrate need and relevance that outweigh the costs and burdens of retrieving and processing the electronically stored information from such sources, including the disruption of business and information management activities.

9. Absent a showing of special need and relevance, a responding party should not be required to preserve, review, or produce deleted, shadowed, fragmented, or residual electronically stored information.

10. A responding party should follow reasonable procedures to protect privileges and objections in connection with the production of electronically stored information.

11. A responding party may satisfy its good faith obligation to preserve and produce relevant electronically stored information by using electronic tools and processes, such as data sampling, searching, or the use of selection criteria, to identify data reasonably likely to contain relevant information.

12. Absent party agreement or court order specifying the form or forms of production, production should be made in the form or forms in which the information is ordinarily maintained or

in a reasonably usable form, taking into account the need to produce reasonably accessible metadata that will enable the receiving party to have the same ability to access, search, and display the information as the producing party where appropriate or necessary in light of the nature of the information and the needs of the case.

13. Absent a specific objection, party agreement or court order, the reasonable costs of retrieving and reviewing electronically stored information should be borne by the responding party, unless the information sought is not reasonably available to the responding party in the ordinary course of business. If the information sought is not reasonably available to the responding party in the ordinary course of business, then, absent special circumstances, the costs of retrieving and reviewing such electronic information may be shared by or shifted to the requesting party.

14. Sanctions, including spoliation findings, should be considered by the court only if it finds that there was a clear duty to preserve, a culpable failure to preserve and produce relevant electronically stored information, and a reasonable probability that the loss of the evidence has materially prejudiced the adverse party.

Go to *www.thesedonaconference.org* to download a free copy of the complete document for your personal use only.

There have been a number of recent cases that have cited to The Sedona Conference Principles in support of discovery issues. Although the collaboration that created the principles is a relatively new concept in the industry, the legal community is adopting them as standard e-discovery best practices.

APPENDIX B

Protecting Yourself Prior to a Lawsuit

Safeguarding work product

You must not wipe data from your drives or otherwise tamper with potential electronic evidence once litigation becomes likely, you are under investigation or a lawsuit has been served. Lawyers may want to consider protecting their work product that is not considered evidence.

If not in the midst of a litigation hold, if you share documents with others in electronic form you may want to consider metadata wiping programs as a proactive way to shield prying eyes from their thought processes. This will allow you to rid files of the remnants of your tracked changes, versions and other historical artifacts. Data wiping should clearly not to be used when you are the target of an investigation or a lawsuit, nor can it be used once litigation has begun or spoliation letters have been sent.

Microsoft itself now offers a complementary metadata wiping program. It does not work on all versions of Office, but it may work for you.

http://www.microsoft.com/downloads/details.
aspx?FamilyID=144e54ed-d43e-42ca-bc7b-5446d34e5360&di
splaylang=en

Another favorite of the legal community is Payne Consulting's

Metadata Assistant. This will allow you to wipe the versioning, track changes, reset the edit time and wipe the author of a document. It also wipes hyperlinks, which can give opposing counsel a peek into how you organize your firm's data. This is a fantastic product to use, even to look at documents that have been provided to you by the other side to see what metadata data hides within. Find the enterprise version of this product on the following site:

http://payneconsulting.com/products/metadataent/

Wiping your computer

It is true that everything you type into your computer or view from the web on your computer can find its way to your hard drive permanently. This means your online chat, your Yahoo and Google e-mail, your bank account password and the confidential client documents that you are drafting or reviewing can resurface. Before you become the target of legal proceedings, consider setting up a wiping program on your PC to clean out those data closets. This will also minimize the damage to you, your company or your clients should your PC be stolen.

Accessdata *(www.accessdata.com)* has a product called SecureClean to permanently erase your leftover data. They also have a whole-disk wiper, which is useful prior to donating a computer.

BC-Wipe is a shareware version of a wiping program. Use a wiping program prior to donating your computer or returning your leased computer. It is the equivalent of shredding your documents before disposing of them. You can find shareware at sites like *www.tucows.com.*

Protecting your company

Prior to initiating any wiping programs, it's important to ensure these practices are in compliance with your company's or firm's document retention policy. This policy should dictate how ESI is managed from the point of creation through destruction, with exceptions for litigation holds and legal purposes. A well-written document retention policy that is implemented, monitored and regularly enforced can dramatically reduce your exposure, especially when discussing "Safe Harbor" in the early "meet and confer" discovery conferences.

APPENDIX C

How to Learn More

Here are some low or no-cost ways to continue your education about e-discovery:

1. Look for supersites:

> *www.discoveryresources.org*
> A compendium of white papers, news and jobs involving e-discovery

> *www.e-discoverylaw.com*
> A database of case law and articles focused on e-discovery published by Kirkpatrick & Lockhart Preston Gates Ellis, LLP.

> *www.law.com/jsp/legaltechnology/index.jsp*
> The legal technology section on law.com

> *http://www.law.cornell.edu/rules/frcp/*
> The online version of the Federal Rules of Civil Procedure

> *http://www.denniskennedy.com/blog/*
> Dennis Kennedy on Legal Technology with a healthy dose of e-discovery

2. Attend conferences and go to classes:

> *www.legaltechshow.com*
> New York is the largest show

www.abanet.org/techshow/
One of the oldest conferences

www.americanconference.com
Industry specific e-discovery conferences

www.acc.com
Association of Corporate Counsel

www.iltanet.org/
Largest conference for litigation support professionals

www.iqpc.com
Industry specific e-discovery conferences

3. Read the books (See the bookstore on discoveryresources.org for a one-stop shop):

Litigation Readiness: An Executive Primer, Prashant Dubey
www.fiosinc.com/resources/books.html

Discovery of Electronically Stored Information: Surveying the Legal Landscape, Ronald J. Hedges
www.bna.com

Essentials of e-Discovery: Finding and Using Electronic Data, Joan Feldman
www.forensics.com/html/whats_new_books_cle. html#EED_description

e-Discovery and Evidence, Michael Arkfeld
arkfeld.com/publication.htm

e-Discovery Law and Practice, Adam Cohen and David Lender

Electronic Evidence, Alan M. Gahtan

Hacking Exposed: Computer Forensics, Davis, Phillips, Cowen

e-Discovery for Corporate Counsel, Mack and Basri, West Publishing (to be published in the 2nd half of 2008)

e-Discovery (Tom Allman's PLI book to be published in 2008)

4. Attend the webcasts

Fios, Inc.

www.fiosinc.com/events/webcasts/

Association of Corporate Counsel
www.acc.com/php/cms/index.php?id=5

American Bar Association
www.abanet.org/cle/

International Legal Technology Association
www.iltanet.org/

5. Ask for demos from providers or visit colleagues and take a tour.

6. Read the case law (posted at discoveryresources.org):

Zubulake I, Zubulake v. UBS Warburg LLC, 217 F.R.D. 309 (S.D.N.Y., 2003)

Zubulake II, Zubulake v. UBS Warburg LLC, 230 F.R.D. 290 (S.D.N.Y., 2003)

Zubulake III, Zubulake v. UBS Warburg LLC, 216 F.R.D. 280 (S.D.N.Y., 2003)

Zubulake IV, Zubulake v. UBS Warburg LLC, 220 F.R.D 212 (S.D.N.Y., 2003)

Zubulake V, Zubulake v. UBS Warburg LLC, 229 F.R.D. 422 (S.D.N.Y., 2004)

Residential Funding Corp. v. DeGeorge Fin. Corp., 306 F.3d 99 (2d Cir. 2002)

Arthur Andersen LLP v. U.S., 544 U.S. 696 (2005)

Coleman (Parent) Holdings, Inc. v. Morgan Stanley & Co., Inc., 2005 WL 679071 (Fla.Cir.Ct. 2005) (aka Perelman v. Morgan Stanley)

Williams v. Sprint/United Mgt.Co., 230 F.R.D. 640 (D. Kan., 2005)

Lorraine v. Markel Am. Ins. Co., 241 F.R.D. (D.Md. 2007)

Bell Atlantic Corp. v. Twombly, 550 U.S. ___, 127 S.Ct. 1955, 167 L.Ed.2d 929 (2007)

Qualcomm, Inc. v. Broadcom Corporation, No. 05-CV-1958-B(BLM), 2008 WL 66932 (S.D. Cal. Jan. 7, 2008)

Victor Stanley, Inc. v. Creative Pipe, Inc. 2008 WL 2221841 (D.Md. May 29, 2008)

In Re Intel Corp. Microprocessor Antitrust Litig., 2008 WL 2310288 (D.Del. June 4, 2008)

7. Follow the e-discovery standards organizations:

The Sedona Conference, *www.thesedonaconference.org*
Industry professionals, attorneys and judges

e-Discovery Reference Model, *www.edrm.net*
Standards committee formed by Socha-Gelbmann

8. Read the blogs (see the blog community on discoveryresources.org)

Dennis Kennedy, *www.denniskennedy.com*
Legal technology in general

Ken Withers, *www.kenwithers.com*
Educating the federal judiciary on e-discovery, state and the new Federal Rules – Ken is now at Sedona, but his website is a historical treasure trove.

Sound Evidence, *DiscoveryResources.org*
Blog for the e-discovery community

Ben Edelman, *www.benedelman.org*
Harvard law student expert witness on Internet and spyware issues

http://sochaconsulting.com
George Socha's compendium of all things e-discovery

http://www.eddupdate.com/
ALM's Monica Bay moderates some of the top experts collaborating on e-discovery

http://www.e-discoverynavigator.com/
Michael Eng's e-discovery blog

http://ralphlosey.wordpress.com/
e-Discovery Team

APPENDIX D

Switching Vendors in the Middle of a Case

Sometimes, by design or necessity, you must move data from vendor to vendor during an e-discovery project. At risk are chain of custody, authenticity of data and critical time. Optimally, this eventuality will be considered and planned for during the contracting part of the project.

When it becomes clear that you must change vendors, talk with of the designated contacts separately to address any issues, substantive or emotional, that may arise. Consider a joint teleconference to introduce the designated contacts and to set the context of this new alliance so that data can be transferred without impacting timelines or authenticity. Provide both of your vendors with written lists of what you are expecting.

For example, you will need, for yourself and your new vendor:

▶ A copy of the chain of custody for the media you sent them

▶ A listing of any manipulation done to the data on the media, if anything other than the original data is to be used by the new vendor

▶ An inventory of what is being shipped

▶ A shipping number and carrier for the data

▶ A contact name and number for issue resolution

The new vendor should immediately unpack and verify the contents of the shipment, making formal note of any discrepancies. The contents of the media should be verified. It is not uncommon for media to be unreadable. Metadata should be checked, particularly date metadata, to make sure the data was transferred using evidence quality copy measures. These are problems to be resolved in the first week of a data transfer.

You may consider requesting that the first vendor retain copies of your materials for a period of time to ensure a safe handoff.

While no vendor wants to see their data shipped to another vendor, it does happen. Professional vendors will make the experience as stress free as possible for their client.

APPENDIX E

e-Discovery Templates

In using the following template, please keep in mind that "less is more." Pick and choose from what is presented here to match the specifics of your case and jurisdiction. These are "kitchen sink" requests, which are appropriate for the most extreme types of e-discovery requests, where spoliation is likely and in criminal matters. You will want to pare these down for normal commercial matters, deploy them as is and/or negotiate them down during your pre-trial conferences.

Asking for more than you need may cause a judge to disallow your requests or award costs. It can also open you up to being asked for the same type and form of information. Past practice was to send a kitchen sink spoliation letter to set up an opponent for sanctions for deletions. In today's climate, practice is to send a preservation request or a description of preservation undertaken to safeguard or remove safe harbor (FRCP 37(e)) protection.

Soft copies of these templates are available at *www.fiosinc.com*.

Form Preservation Letter to Opposing Counsel – "Meet & Confer"

Dear ____,

We look forward to our meet and confer session where we will, among other things, discuss preservation. Until we come to an agreement or receive a court order regarding the scope of preservation, we expect that your client ____ will suspend any automatic deletions, purging or overwriting for ESI applicable to the instant case.

We are particularly concerned that the following ESI may be deleted and expect that you and your client will establish a coherent legal hold for transaction data for [subject], e-mail [chat, dynamic web pages, logs].

Our client will be preserving the appropriate content stores via the following protocols:

1. Legal holds were issued to key custodians and IT, followed up by training and monitoring.

2. A backup tape set was taken out of rotation on [date]. We intend to continue our tape rotation policy which will overwrite tapes in the normal course of business.

3. Departing employees data in the following divisions will be saved.

4. We do not save chat and have a policy against using home computers for business.

5. We delete voice mail at [ ] days and will continue to do so.

6. We have various proprietary applications that summarize data and delete the detail. We are analyzing those systems for applicability and once we determine the system is applicable, we will design, develop and implement a way to save the detail records in a way that does not impact business.

We trust you will view these efforts as our good faith approach to litigating this case on the merits. We believe this is a balanced, reasonable preservation. Should you wish more preserved, we are open to discussing and expect that your client will be open to underwriting costs.

We look forward to litigating on the merits.

Best regards,

xxxx

Sample Form Legal Hold or Preservation Letter Letter to Employees

Highly Confidential, Attorney Client Communication

Acknowledgment required

Date:

Addressee:

Re: [Code name for legal hold]

Dear _____:

We need your help on a matter critical to the company. It is a legal matter, so there are certain protocols which must be honored.

The contents of this letter are privileged, under attorney client communication. This means the contents will not need to be disclosed to the legal opposition. You are not to discuss this letter with anyone, except [your manager], the coordinator listed at the bottom of this letter or someone designated by them. If you do discuss this letter or the actions you take with others, you may dilute or remove the privilege and be subject to deposition or testimony from our legal opponent.

Please acknowledge via e-mail that you understand and will comply with the guidelines set forth in this letter regarding the obligation you have to save the material identified below.

Saving material is sometimes referred to as a "legal hold" or "preservation." It is a legal obligation which we must satisfy or it will expose [corporation] to enormous risk. Employees who do not comply will be subject to [disciplinary action, discharge, criminal prosecution.] In addition, compliance with this letter will be part of your quarterly review for bonus purpose.

The subject matter of the material to be saved is: [describe in particularity — communications and work papers regarding a particular project, company, product...]. The applicable time period is from [start date] to [finish date]. The company [does/does not] have an ongoing obligation to save material as it is created or received.

On a practical level, this means that you should not delete any e-mails [or voice mails] [you send or receive on this topic, or that you have sent or received in the past]. If you need space in your e-mail box, you must archive your e-mail and save the resulting file to your home directory on the network, according to the technical instructions attached to this e-mail. You should not erase or throw out any disks, memory sticks, CD's or paper documents containing the targeted subject matter.

Do not erase files on your desktop, laptop, pda, home drive, files in network shares, and documents in document management systems or records in databases like customer management systems, job ordering systems [or other systems of interest].

Do not throw out or shred your paper files.

Please notify the coordinator identified below if:

▶ You have any questions about this letter

▶ You are not sure whether you should save or purge a particular document

▶ You are not sure how or where to save the material

▶ You are not sure we've covered all electronic systems where data about { code name} might reside.

▶ You have pertinent documents in a document management system which might be deleted automatically due to normal retention

▶ You are concerned that saving the data will impact the performance of computer systems

▶ Your computer needs service

▶ You get a new computer

▶ You change jobs

▶ You leave the company

▶ You hire anyone who will also handle material covered by this letter.

▶ You receive any instructions, written or verbal, which contradict this letter.

It is the stated intent of [corporation] to discharge our obligation to safeguard this information until further notice. While some might think that it could help [corporation] to destroy material, it actually will hurt [corporation] and submit you to [disciplinary action/criminal prosecution/loss of bonus].

The coordinator for [Code name for legal hold] is [Inside Counsel attorney, outside counsel or point person]. Their e-mail is xxx@company.com and phone is 555.555.5555 [or special 800 number].

We will notify you when you are no longer under this obligation. We may interview you or your manager over the next two weeks to further fine tune the preservation obligation.

Thank you in advance for your cooperation.

Sincerely,

[Joe Smith, [Technology Counsel]

cc: Jane Doe [CEO]
    Bill Jones [General Counsel]
    Bill Smith [Huey, Dewey and Long, counsel to the Corporation]

Older Form Preservation Letter to Opposing Counsel

[date]

[address]

re: [matter (, case caption)]

Dear: _____,

By this letter, you and your client{s} are hereby given notice not to destroy, conceal or alter any paper or electronically stored information (ESI) generated by or under the control of your client {clients} . Until we narrow the preservation obligation by agreement or otherwise, we expect that you will preserve any potentially responsive ESI.

As you know, your client's {clients'} failure to comply with this notice can result in severe sanctions being imposed by the Court {and liability in tort} for spoliation of evidence or potential evidence.

{Although [we may bring/have brought] a motion for an order preserving documents and things from destruction or alteration, your client's {clients'} obligation to preserve documents and things for discovery in this case arises in law and equity independently from any order on such motion.}

Consider carefully whether to request forensics as you may need to pay for it.

{Our discovery requests [ask/will ask] for certain data on the hard disks, floppy disks and backup media used in your client's {clients'} computers, some of which data are not readily available to an ordinary computer user, such as "deleted" files and "file fragments." As you may know, although a user may "erase" or "delete" a file, all that is really erased is a reference to that file in a table on the hard disk; unless overwritten with new data, a "deleted" file can be as intact on the disk as any "active" file you would see in a directory listing.}

{If there are particular items of ESI which are key to your case, you may want to pick and choose from the following lists of ESI}

Accordingly, electronic data and storage media that may be subject to our discovery requests and that your client{s} are obligated to maintain and not alter or destroy, include but are not limited to the following:

Introduction: description of files and file types sought

All digital or analog electronic files, including "deleted" files and file fragments, stored in machine-readable format on magnetic, optical or other storage media, including the hard drives or floppy disks used by your client's {clients'} computers and their backup media (e.g., other hard drives, backup tapes, floppies, Jaz cartridges, thumb drives, IPods, and other personal storage devices like DVD's and CD-ROMs) or otherwise, whether such files have been reduced to paper printouts or not. More specifically, your client{s} is {are} to preserve all of your e-mails, both sent and received, whether internally or externally; all word-processed files, including drafts and revisions; all spreadsheets, including drafts and revisions; all databases; all CAD (computer-aided design) files, including drafts and revisions; all presentation data or slide shows produced by presentation software (such as Microsoft PowerPoint); all graphs, charts and other data produced by project management software (such as Microsoft Project); all data generated by calendaring, task management and personal information management (PIM) software (such as Microsoft Outlook or Lotus Notes); all data created with the use of personal data assistants (PDAs), such as PalmPilot, Blackberry, or other Windows CE-based or Pocket PC devices; all data created with the use of document management software or Customer Relationship Management (CRM) software; all data created with the use of paper and electronic mail logging and routing software; all Internet and Web-browser-generated history files, caches and "cookies" files generated at the workstation of each employee and/or agent in your client's {clients'} employ and on any and all backup storage media; and any and all other files generated by users through the use of computers and/or telecommunications, including but not limited to voice mail.

We also seek information under the control of your client{clients} such as web based e-mail like Yahoo or gmail, social networking sites, application services providers like Salesforce.com, the electronic records of service providers like ADP, Visa, and UPS.

Further, you are to preserve any log or logs of network use by employees or otherwise, whether kept in paper or electronic form, and to preserve all copies of your backup tapes and the software necessary to reconstruct the data on those tapes. We may request complete, bit-by-bit "mirror" evidentiary image copy of the storage media of each and every personal computer (and/or workstation) and network server in your control and custody containing material potentially responsive in this matter, as well as image copies of all hard drives retained by you and no longer in service, including storage used by terminated employees, in use at any time from _____ to the present.

Your client{s} is {are} also not to pack, compress, purge or otherwise dispose of files and parts of files unless a true and correct copy of such files is made.}

Your client{s} is {are} also to preserve and not destroy all passwords, decryption procedures (including, if necessary, the software to decrypt the files); network access codes, ID names, manuals, tutorials, written instructions, decompression or reconstruction software, and any and all other information and things necessary to access, view and (if necessary) reconstruct the electronic data we [are requesting/will request] through discovery.

We make ourselves available at your earliest convenience to meet and confer regarding narrowing the required preservation and setting the dates for subsequent discussions to define and narrow productions, agree on privilege handling and other matters toward a swift and just resolution of our clients' differences.

Formal verbiage to narrow preservation request

1. Business Records: [All documents and information about documents containing backup and/or archive policy and/or procedure, document retention policy, names of backup and/or archive software, names and addresses of any offsite storage provider, records management and enterprise content management systems]. [between the following dates]. [at the following locations]. [in the following departments]. [about the following issues].

   a. All e-mail and information about e-mail (including message contents, header information and logs of e-mail system usage) {sent or received} by the following persons:

      [list names, job titles]

   b. All other e-mail and information about e-mail (including message contents, header information and logs of e-mail system usage) containing information about or related to:

      [insert detail]

   c. All databases (including all records and fields and structural information in such databases), containing any reference to and/or information about or related to:

      [insert detail]

   d. All logs of activity (both in paper and electronic formats) on computer systems and networks that have or may have been used to process or store electronic data containing information about or related to:

[insert detail]

e. All word processing files, including prior drafts, archived copies, "deleted" files and file fragments, containing information about or related to:

[insert detail]

f. With regard to electronic data created by application programs which process financial, accounting and billing information, all electronic data files, including prior drafts, archived copies, "deleted" files and file fragments, containing information about or related to:

[insert detail]

g. All files, including prior drafts, archived copies, "deleted" files and file fragments, containing information from electronic calendars and scheduling programs regarding or related to:

[insert detail]

h. All electronic data files, including prior drafts, archived copies, "deleted" files and file fragments about or related to:

[insert detail]

2. Online Data Storage on Network Attached Storage, Mainframes and Minicomputers: With regard to online storage and/or direct access storage devices attached to your client's {clients'} mainframe computers and/or minicomputers: they are not to modify or delete any electronic data files, archived copies, "deleted" files and file fragments existing at the time of this letter's delivery, which meet the definitions set forth in this letter, unless a true and correct copy of each such electronic data file has been made and steps have been taken to assure that such a copy will be preserved and accessible for purposes of this litigation.

3. Offline Data Storage, Backups and Archives, Floppy Diskettes, Tapes and Other Removable Electronic Media: With regard to

all electronic media used for offline storage, including magnetic tapes and cartridges and other media that, at the time of this letter's delivery, contained any electronic data meeting the criteria listed in paragraph 1 above: Your client {clients} is {are} to stop any activity that may result in the loss of such electronic data, including rotation, destruction, overwriting and/or erasure of such media in whole or in part. This request is intended to cover all removable electronic media used for data storage in connection with their computer systems, including magnetic tapes and cartridges, magneto-optical disks, floppy diskettes and all other media, whether used with servers, personal computers, minicomputers or mainframes or other computers, and whether containing backup and/or archive data sets and other electronic data, for all of their computer systems.

4. Replacement of Data Storage Devices: Your client {clients} is {are} not to dispose of any electronic data storage devices and/or media that may be replaced due to failure and/or upgrade and/or other reasons that may contain electronic data meeting the criteria listed in paragraph 1 above.

5. Fixed Drives on Stand-Alone Personal Computers and Network Workstations: With regard to electronic data meeting the criteria listed in paragraph 1 above, which existed on fixed drives attached to stand-alone microcomputers and/or network workstations at the time of this letter's delivery: Your client {clients} is {are} not to alter or erase such electronic data, and not to perform other procedures (such as data compression and disk de-fragmentation or optimization routines) that may impact such data, unless a true and correct copy has been made of such active files and of completely restored versions of such deleted electronic files and file fragments, copies have been made of all directory listings (including hidden files) for all directories and subdirectories containing such files, and arrangements have been made to preserve copies during the pendency of this litigation.

6. Programs and Utilities: Your client {clients} is {are} to preserve copies of all application programs and utilities, which may be used to process electronic data covered by this letter.

7. Log of System Modifications: Your client {clients} is {are} to

maintain an activity log to document modifications made to any electronic data processing system that may affect the system's capability to process any electronic data meeting the criteria listed in paragraph 1 above, regardless of whether such modifications were made by employees, contractors, vendors and/or any other third parties.

8. Personal Computers Used by Your Employees and/or Their Secretaries and Assistants: The following steps should immediately be taken in regard to all personal computers used by your client's {clients'} employees and/or their secretaries and assistants.

   a. As to fixed drives attached to such computers: (i) a true and correct copy is to be made of all electronic data on such fixed drives relating to this matter, including all active files and completely restored versions of all deleted electronic files and file fragments; (ii) full directory listings (including hidden files) for all directories and subdirectories (including hidden directories) on such fixed drives should be written; and (iii) such copies and listings are to be preserved until this matter reaches its final resolution.

   b. All floppy diskettes, magnetic tapes and cartridges, and other media used in connection with such computers prior to the date of delivery of this letter containing any electronic data relating to this matter are to be collected and put into storage for the duration of this lawsuit.

9. Evidence Created Subsequent to This Letter: With regard to electronic data created subsequent to the date of delivery of this letter, relevant evidence is not be destroyed and your client {clients} is {are} to take whatever steps are appropriate to avoid destruction of evidence.

In order to assure that your and your client's {clients'} obligation to preserve documents and things will be met, please forward a copy of this letter to all persons and entities with custodial responsibility for the items referred to in this letter. We expect that you will monitor compliance.

Sincerely, etc.

Sample e-Discovery Interrogatories and Requests for Production

Below are sample interrogatories and requests for production that are meant to be complementary (i.e., any devices or electronic files that are identified in answer to an interrogatory or interrogatories are usually immediately requested in the follow-up request[s] for production). Use these to prepare your 30(b)(6) person most knowledgeable.

For each of these questions, consider making the most narrow request possible, while at the same time, being forthcoming.

Sample Interrogatories and Requests for Production

[Note: The precise format for the following suggested interrogatories and requests for production of documents and things should be in accordance with the applicable civil and local rules of the court where the matter is filed.]

[suggested language for inclusion in preamble:]

I. Definitions

For the purposes of the following interrogatories and requests for production of documents and things, the following definitions apply:

Application Software: A set of electronic instructions, also known as a program, which instructs a computer to perform a specific set of processes.

Archive: A copy of data on a computer drive, or on a portion of a drive, maintained for historical reference.

Backup: A copy of active data, intended for use in restoration of data.

Computer: Includes but is not limited to network servers, desktops, laptops, notebook computers, employees' home computers, mainframes, the PDAs of [party name] and its employees (personal digital assistants, such as PalmPilot, Blackberry and other such handheld computing devices), digital cell phones, smartphones and pagers.

Data: Any and all information stored on media that may be accessed by a computer.

Digital Camera: A camera that stores still or moving pictures in a digital format (jpg, GIF, etc.).

Document: Includes but is not limited to any electronically stored data on magnetic or optical storage media as an "active" file or files (readily readable by one or more computer applications or forensics software); any "deleted" but recoverable electronic files on said media; any electronic file fragments (files that have been deleted and partially overwritten with new data); and slack (data fragments stored randomly from random access memory on a hard drive during the normal operation of a computer [RAM slack] or residual data left on the hard drive after new data has overwritten some but not all of previously stored data).

ESI: Electronically Stored Information

FRCP: Federal Rules of Civil Procedure

Hard Drive: The primary hardware that a computer uses to store information, typically magnetized media on rotating disks.

Help Features/Documentation: Instructions that assist a user on how to set up and use a product including but not limited to software, manuals and instruction files.

Imaged Copy: A "mirror image" bit-by-bit copy of a hard drive (i.e., a complete replication of the physical drive).

Input Device: Any object that allows a user to communicate with a computer by entering information or issuing commands (e.g., keyboard, mouse or joystick).

Magnetic or Optical Storage Media: Include but are not limited to hard drives (also known as "hard disks"), backup tapes, CD-ROMs, DVD-ROMs, JAZ and Zip drives, smart cards, memory sticks, digital jukeboxes, and floppy disks.

Network: A group of connected computers that allow people to share information and equipment (e.g., local area network [LAN], wide area network [WAN], metropolitan area network [MAN], storage area network [SAN], peer-to-peer network, client-server network).

Operating System: Software that directs the overall activity of a computer (e.g., MS-DOS, Windows, Linux).

Network Operating System: Software that directs the overall activity of networked computers.

Software: Any set of instructions stored on computer-readable media that tells a computer what to do. Includes operating systems and applications.

Storage Devices: Any device that a computer uses to store information.

Storage Media: Storage media are any removable devices that store data.

For each of the following, please answer the question or produce the requested material for either

The following named people: {Person 1, Person 2, Person 3 } and any person with the same or similar job duties to the listed personnel, those persons' managers and direct reports.

The following named departments: {Accounting, Sales, Marketing}

Persons or departments working on the following project or subject matter

From the dates _____ to _____.

In the following locations: _____

II. Spoliation: getting information on preservation of information.

S1. Written policies on preservation of records

Interrogatory No._____:

Do you have a written policy for the retention of documents, including but not limited to business records?

Request for Production No._____:

Please produce copies of any and all written policies for the retention of documents, for the time period of _____ to _____ _____ inclusive.

S2. Destruction of documents

Interrogatory No._____:

Do you have a written policy for the destruction of documents, including but not limited to business records?

Request for Production No._____:

Please produce copies of any and all written policies for the destruction of documents, for the time period of _____ to ___ _____ inclusive.

Interrogatory No._____:

Has destruction or overwriting of documents been suspended in writing? If so, please provide a copy of any notices, follow-ups and acknowledgements.

S3. Persons in charge of maintaining document retention and destruction policies

Interrogatory No._____:

Identified by job title, job description and business address and telephone number, who are all persons in charge of implementing the policies identified in your answer to Interrogatories 1, 2 and 3 above?

Interrogatory No._____ :

If not the same person(s) as identified in your answer to the immediately preceding interrogatory, identify by job title, job description, and business address and telephone number, the person at [party name] who is the most knowledgeable about the retention and destruction of documents at [party name]?

Interrogatory No._____:

With respect to preventing the destruction, accidental or otherwise, of documents and things that may potentially become evidence in litigation, please identify with particularity and in detail:

    a. Whether the minutes of the meetings of the Board of Directors, from [date] to [date] contain any references to considerations or discussions of preventing such destruction of potential evidence.

b. If so, state the dates of the meetings for which minutes were taken.

c. If so, state the name, title, job description, business address and telephone number of the person or persons with custody of those minutes.

Request for Production No._____:

Please produce all documents referenced in the immediately preceding interrogatory.

S4. Preservation of evidence

Interrogatory No._____:

Since [date of opposing party's awareness of client's claim or counterclaim, if not date of complaint, cross-claim or counterclaim], have any documents at [party name] been destroyed? If so, please state which electronic files have been deleted from the media of [party name] or overwritten from that date to the present, and dates of destruction or overwriting.

S5. Storage of documents

Interrogatory No._____:

As to the storage of data generated by the users of your computers (such as word-processed files and e-mail), please state whether:

A. The data are backed up on tape or other media?

    1. If so:

        a. How many such media currently exist with backup data on them?

        b. What is the maximum storage size in megabytes for each such media?

        c. What is the brand name for each such media?

        d. When was the last time each such media was backed up with data?

  e. What was the computer or other hardware (e.g., individual workstation, server) for each such backup?

  f. With respect to the immediately foregoing question, state the physical location and current user of each computer or other hardware listed.

Request for Production No._____:

Please produce all backup and/or archive media, for the time period of _____ to _____ inclusive.

III. Indentifying & Authenticating the Evidence

Interrogatory No._____:

Does or did [party name] maintain, or contract with another party to maintain, an overall inventory of data resources such as a Year 2000 Plan, a 9/11 Recovery Plan or Disaster Recovery Plan? If so, please provide the name, address, phone number and other contact information for the individuals primarily responsible for maintenance of the inventory and/or plan.

Request No._____:

Produce any and all company organizational and policy information in its entirety, including but not limited to organizational charts, corporate policy and procedure manuals, policy memoranda, system schematic, network topology, system restart procedures, e-mail retention policies, Year 2000 Plan, a 9/11 Recovery Plan, Disaster Recovery Plan, and other related items.

IV. Information Technology Personnel

Interrogatory No._____:

Provide a list of all personnel responsible for maintaining computer hardware, data or information systems on computers for [party name]. Include name, position title, contact information, and official job description and list of duties.

Request No._____:

Produce all formal and informal contact lists and duty rosters for personnel in Information Technology (IT) and Information Services (IS), or equivalent divisions within [party name]. Specifically include rosters for groups such as Incident Response Teams, Data Recovery Units, Audit/Investigation Teams, etc.

Request No._____:

Produce all formal job descriptions, assignments and personnel lists for IT and IS personnel, including revisions, for the period _____ to _____.

V. Loose Media (including Backup and Archive)

Interrogatory No._____:

Does [party name] maintain a policy regarding use of loose or removable media in its workstations, computers or networks? If so, state the name of the person(s) responsible for creating and enforcing that policy.

Request No._____:

Provide a copy of the policy mentioned in the preceding interrogatory, as well as any revisions, records or logs related to formulation or enforcement of that policy for the period _____ to _____.

Request No._____:

Produce any and all devices used to place information on loose or removable storage media, including but not limited to hard drives, floppy drives, CD-ROM drives, tape drives, recordable DVD-ROM drives, and removable drives. Include all instructions for use and maintenance of those devices.

Request No._____:

Produce any and all loose or removable media used to store data, including but not limited to floppy disks, CD-ROM discs and tape drive cartridges, that have been used by personnel or contractors of [party name] to perform work for [party name].

Request No._____:

Produce any and all backup and/or archived data [describe scope of data].

VI. Computer Hardware

This is most appropriate for forensics work or when a motion to compel must be used to gather opponent's data.

Interrogatory No._____:

List all computer equipment provided by [party name] or used by employees of [party name] to perform work for [party name], including but not limited to hardware and/or peripherals attached to a computer such as computer cases [desktop, tower, portable/batteries, all-in-one], monitors, modems [internal, external], printers, keyboards, printers, scanners, mice [cord and cordless], pointing devices [joystick, touchpad, trackball] and speakers. Include description of equipment, serial number, all users for the period _____ to _____ and dates used, and all locations where the equipment was located for the period _____ to _____.

Interrogatory No._____:

Will [party name] permit, without an order therefore, inspection of the equipment mentioned in the preceding interrogatory?

Request No. [follow-up, if response to preceding interrogatory is negative] _____:

Please produce the following computers, including their magnetic or optical storage media, for inspection and copying, on or before [date], at the offices of [law firm] at [address]:

[list of computers you want image-copied, previously identified in discovery; alternatively, if you know the computer population is relatively small]:

Please produce your computers, including their magnetic or optical storage media, for inspection and copying, on or before [date], at the offices of [law firm] at [address]:

Interrogatory No._____:

List all hardware components (e.g., motherboard, modem, NIC, etc.) installed internally or externally to the PC(s) used by _____ during the period _____ to _____.

Request No._____:

Provide any and all documentation of software and hardware modifications to the PC(s) used by _____ during the period _____ to _____, including but not limited to modification dates, software/hardware titles and version numbers, names of persons performing modifications, location of any backup of the data on the computer performed prior to modification, and disposition of replaced software and hardware.

Request No._____:

Produce any and all documentation instructing in setup and use of the PC(s) used by _____ during the period _____ to _____, and hardware and software installed on that/those PC(s). Include any and all documentation reflecting communication with a computer professional or help desk for help in setting up and using the PC(s).

Interrogatory No._____:

List discarded or replaced hardware and software for the PC(s) (including entire PCs) used by _____ during the period _____ to _____. If the hardware or software is no longer in your control, then include the name and contact information of last known custodian.

VII. Computer Software

Request No._____:

Produce list of any and all software installed or used on the PC(s) used by _____ during the period ____ to _____. Include all titles and version numbers. Include authors and contact information for authors of custom or customized software. Include operating system(s) associated with each software program.

VIII. Operating Systems

Interrogatory No._____:

List all operating systems (including but not limited to UNIX, Windows, DOS, Linux and PDA operating systems) installed on all computers used by [party name], the specific equipment the OS was installed on and the period during which it was installed on the specific equipment.

Request No._____:

Provide copies of all operating system software listed in the preceding interrogatory, and all supporting documentation provided with the software, and any manuals and tutorials acquired by [party name] to support use of the software.

IX. Telephony

Interrogatory No._____:

Do you have any graphic representation of the components of your telephone and voice messaging system, and the relationship of those components to each other, including but not limited to flow charts, videos or photos, and diagrams?

Interrogatory No._____:

If so, where are the documents located? Include logical paths for electronic documents.

Request No._____:

Produce copies of any and all graphic representations of your telephone and voice messaging network, and the relationship of those components to each other, including any revisions, for the period of _____ to _____ inclusive. If the documents are electronic, please produce them in their native form, as they existed at the time they were drafted, based on archive or back-up data.

Interrogatory No._____:

List all telephone equipment provided by [party name] or used by employees of [party name] to perform work for [party name], including but not limited to desktop telephones, cell phones, pagers, PDA and laptop modems, calling cards, telephony software and contact management software. Include description of equipment and software, serial number, all users for the period of _____ to _____ inclusive and dates used, and all locations where the equipment was located for the period of _____ to _____ inclusive.

Interrogatory No._____:

Will [party name] permit, without an order therefore, inspection of the equipment mentioned in the preceding interrogatory?

Request No._____:

Produce any and all voice messaging records including but not limited to caller message recordings, digital voice recordings, interactive voice response unit (IVR/VRU) recordings, unified messaging files, webcasts, podcasts and computer-based voice mail files to or from [specified parties] for the period ____ to ___.

Request No._____:

Produce all phone use records for [party name] including but not limited to logs of incoming and outgoing calls, invoices and contact management records, manually or automatically created or generated for the period from _____ to _____ inclusive.

X. Other Sources of Electronic Evidence

Interrogatory No._____:

List all log files (files with suffixes) found on computers in [party name]'s network, and the equipment and logical path where the log files may be found.

Request No._____:

Provide copies of the following log files: [this is a follow-up request to the preceding interrogatory, issued after the list of log files has been reviewed]

Request No._____:

Produce any and all manual and automatic records of equipment use, including but not limited to fax, access, audit, security, e-mail, printing, error and transmission records.

Interrogatory No._____:

Do any employees of [party name] subscribe to or participate in Internet newsgroups or chat groups in the course of their employment? If so, list all users and the services that they subscribe to or participate in.

Request No._____:

Produce any and all information related to newsgroups or chat groups, including but not limited to names and passwords for each and every service, newsgroup messages, text files and programs used to access messages.

Interrogatory No._____:

Do any employees of [party name] use portable devices in the course of their employment that are not connected to [party name]'s network, and that are not backed up or archived? If so, list all users and the devices they use.

Request No._____:

Produce any and all portable devices not backed up or archived, including but not limited to handheld devices, set-top boxes, notebook devices, flash drives, cell phones, digital recorders, digital cameras and external storage devices.

Interrogatory No._____:

Does [party name] provide Internet access for any of its employees or has [party name] done so at any time during the period from ____ to ____ inclusive? If so, list the employees who had Internet access, the Internet service provider (ISP) used, and describe the method(s) used to connect to the Internet.

Request No._____:

Produce any and all documentation describing installation and use of hardware and software used by [party name] to provide Internet access for its employees during the period from ____ to ____ inclusive.

Request No._____:

Produce copies of all manuals, policies and other guidelines for employee access and use of Internet resources.

Interrogatory No._____:

Describe any restrictions on, controls over or monitoring of employee use of Internet resources.

Request No._____:

Provide any records generated as a result of restrictions on, controls over and monitoring of employee use of Internet resources.

Interrogatory No._____:

Provide a list of any and all Internet-related data on the PCs used by [specific employees or classes of employees], including but not limited to saved Web pages, lists of Web sites, URL addresses, Web browser software and settings, bookmarks, favorites, history lists, caches, cookies.

XI. Data Security Measures

Interrogatory No._____:

List any and all user identification numbers and passwords necessary to access computers or programs addressed in interrogatories and requests. Your response to this interrogatory must be updated with responses to future sets of interrogatories and requests and updated responses to any set of interrogatories and requests.

Interrogatory No._____:

Please provide copies of your computer security policies and procedures and the name and contact information for the person responsible for security.

Interrogatory No._____:

Please provide information about the security settings for the [program]. For example, please provide the security settings for the Exchange Server, noting who has administrative rights.

XII. Network Questions

Request No._____:

Produce any and all documents and things related to networks or groups of connected computers that allow people to share information and equipment, including but not limited to local area networks (LANs), wide area networks (WANs), metropolitan area networks (MANs), storage area networks (SANs), peer-to-peer networks, client-server networks, integrated services digital networks, virtual networks, cloud computing and VPNs.

Request No._____:

Produce any and all components related to networks, including but not limited to information exchange components (e.g., Ethernet, token-ring, ATM), network work file servers, traffic, hubs, network interface cards, cables, firewalls, user names, passwords and intranet. (useful for network intrusion and cybercrime).

N1. System overview

Interrogatory No._____:

Do you have any graphic representation of the components of your computer network, and the relationship of those components to each other, including but not limited to flow charts, videos or photos, and drawings? Include network topology documents and network schemas in your response.

Interrogatory No._____:

If so, where are the documents located? Include logical paths and physical locations for electronic representations.

Request No._____:

Produce copies of any and all graphic representations of your computer network, and the relationship of those components to each other, including any revisions, for the period of _____ to _____ _ inclusive. If the documents are electronic, produce them in their native form, as they existed at the time they were drafted, based on version or backup data.

XIII. Electronic Mail (e-mail)

Request No._____:

Produce any and all information related to e-mail, including but not limited to current, backed-up and archived programs, accounts, unified messaging, server-based e-mail, web-based e-mail, dial-up e-mail, user names and addresses, domain names and addresses, e-mail messages, attachments, manual and automated mailing lists and mailing list addresses.

APPENDIX F

Sample Fact Witness and 30(b)(6) Deposition Questions

Questions to Ask or Prepare the 30(b)(6) Deposition of Corporate IT Person

The following questions may be useful to ask of or prepare a deponent in order to track down the sources of electronic data relevant to your case. The broad non-technical questions serve as a foundation for more technical questions, and many can also be used with less-technical witnesses. Not all of these questions will be relevant in all situations, and the ideal amount of follow-up depends greatly on the specific facts, issues, and witnesses with which the legal team is working.

Depending on the jurisdiction's limitation on interrogatories, most of the following questions can be used first in interrogatories, with follow-ups wherever necessary in depositions and requests for production. You may wish to have an e-discovery expert prepare you and/or your witness in prior to asking or answering these questions. An e-discovery expert can also help you assess the transcribed responses that were given by witnesses in prior depositions for completeness and accuracy.

Under the revised Federal Rules of Civil Procedure, it may also be useful to exchange answers to some or all of these questions as part of the mandatory meet and confer negotiations between counsel. To the extent that questions can be answered through that mechanism, the legal team will have greater background information to explore at deposition and perhaps a reduced need to use interrogatories that could then be used for substantive development of the case.

When providing these answers, it may be better to provide them in writing, so that ambiguity can be resolved in a controlled manner and consistent answers can be given across matters when the same systems are involved. You can start your answer bank with your first 26(f) preparation or 30(b)(6) deposition.

Personnel

1. What is your title and job responsibilities?

2. Are you a member of a formal department?

3. Who else is in the department?

4. To whom at your company do you report?

5. Who works directly under you?

6. Does your company have an organizational chart? Who has custody of such a chart?

7. How many people at your company have a direct responsibility for computers and/or networks?

8. What are their job titles and duties?

9. Where are they located, if not at your location?

10. What outsourced services, if any, do you use in the care and maintenance of your company's computer hardware, software or network(s)?

11. Who is the person at your company who is ultimately responsible for responding to discovery requests made of your attorney(s) in this lawsuit?

12. Does this person have the same responsibility for any other lawsuits?

13. If you are not that person, what role, if any, did you

play in responding to discovery requests made of your attorney(s) in this lawsuit?

14. What have you done to prepare for your deposition here today?

15. What documents did you review prior to your deposition here today?

System information

1. Do you personally use a computer or computers at work? If so, how many?

    a. Is the computer on your desk?

    b. Is it a desktop or a laptop computer?

    c. Do you know the brand name?

    d. Does it run on Windows?

        – If so, Windows 3.1, 95, 98, 2000, NT, XP or Vista?

        – If not, is it a Unix-based system? Linux? Macintosh? Apple?

2. Are you the only person with access to this computer?

    a. If not, who else uses it?

    b. Who else has access to it?

    c. Do you know whether this computer has ever been used in the past by anyone else?

    d. If so, who?

    e. When and where was your computer bought?

    f. Who keeps the records of computer equipment purchases, including your computer?

    g. Does your computer have a hard drive?

        – Does it have more than one?

– Do you know the storage capacity in gigabytes, of the hard drive(s) in your computer? If so, what is it?

h. Do you need to use a password to access the computer?

– Did you set the password yourself, or was it issued to you?

– How often do you change the password?

– Does anyone else in your company know your password?

i. Does the computer have a floppy disk drive? A CD-ROM drive? USB ports?

j. Have you ever accessed your work computer from another location? If so, when? What did you access? Did you save any files? If so, to what media?

k. Are you able to save files on your computer to an external device? Have you ever done this?

l. Does your computer have any remote access software installed on it? Have you ever accessed your computer remotely?

m. Can your computer connect to the Internet and send and receive e-mail?

n. Do you ever make a backup copy of files stored on your computer?

1. How often do you make backup copies?

2. Do you use backup software or just copy files to other storage media?

3. Do you keep multiple backup copies?

4. How long do you retain a backup copy?

5. How do you recycle or destroy old backup copies?

6. Is there any company policy about creating and retaining personal backups?

o. Do you ever make "personal" copies of files or other data from your computer (work station)?

1. When do you do so, and how often?

2. What process do you use to create "personal" copies?

3. Where do you store personal copies after you have created them? Do you upload them to a home computer?

p. Do you use more than one work-issued computer? How do you transfer files and synchronize computer information between the two?

q. Do you use a smartphone, Blackberry, Sidekick or other PDA for work?

1. Do you synchronize that with all your work computers?

2. Do you synchronize it with any home computers?

a. Do you use a computer at home? [if so, repeat relevant questions above as to type, kind, features, backups, who else has access to it, etc.]

r. Have you received or sent work-related e-mail from your home computer?

s. Have you used your home computer to do work for your company?

t. Has your employer paid for all or a part of your home computer, smartphone, or PDA?

Network Information

1. Is the computer you use at work connected to a network?

a. Do you know the type of network it is (LAN, WAN, intranet)?

b. Do you have any administrator or special access

rights on the network?

    c. Are there any parts of the network that you cannot access?

2. Please describe your computer setup at work.

    a. Do you need a password to get onto the network? Is it the same as the password you use to log onto your computer?

    b. Does anyone else know your network password?

    c. Have you heard of computer servers, which are also called file servers and network servers?

    d. Does your network have any servers on it? More than one?

    e. What kind of network do you have (e.g., Microsoft, Novell, Lotus Notes, Unix, Linux)?

    f. Do you have an I.T. person whose primary responsibility is keeping the network and its servers running smoothly (sometimes known as a network administrator)?   If not, whose job is that?

    g. Is there an Information Services or Information Technology department in your company? What are the names of those people and who is the person in charge?

    h. Is there somebody in charge of backing up data from the server? If so, who?

    i. Do you know whether a backup system is in place? Do you know how often the network server is backed up?

    j. Do you know what kind of backup hardware and software are used? If so, what specific hardware and software, and version of that software? If not: who would most likely know the answers to this question?

    k. What is your understanding as to how your

company's computer data will be preserved in the event of a disaster, such as a fire, flood, theft or vandalism? Are you familiar with the phrases "business continuity" or "disaster recovery?"

E-mail Usage

1. Do you send and receive e-mail from your computer? If so, what e-mail program(s) do you use? (If he/she does not know, suggest Microsoft Outlook, Outlook Express, Thunderbird, Lotus Notes, Eudora, Novell Groupwise as possibilities).

2. Do you use any internet-based e-mail services like AOL, Gmail, Hotmail, or Yahoo! Mail for business purposes?

   a. If so, how long have you been doing that?

   b. Do other people at your company also use internet-based e-mail for business purposes? How do you keep track of e-mail addresses?

3. Do you know whether your e-mail messages are kept on an e-mail server, on your computer, or both? Can you read the e-mail on your computer when you're disconnected from the network or from the internet?

4. Does your company use any tools to log incoming and/or outgoing mail? (If unclear mention "Sarbanes compliance.") If not, is there a policy on how incoming mail is logged and routed?

5. What do you do with e-mail messages after you have read them? Do you put them into folders? Do you delete them?

6. If you save your e-mail messages, do you ever get messages that you have run out of storage space? How often has this happened? How is this problem solved? Does this ever make you delete messages you had wanted to save?

7. Do you know if your e-mail is backed up from time to time by I.T., either from your desktop computer or from the network server?

8. Have you ever printed out an e-mail message? If so, how often, when, and for what purpose?

9. Have you ever archived your e-mail? If so, how? Have you ever heard of a "PST" file? Do you have any of those?

Other Software Usage

1. What other software programs do you use at work?

   a. What word processing software do you use?

      i. Have you ever used different software for this purpose while at this company?

         1. *If yes, how long ago?*

         2. *If yes, did you keep any files created back then?*

         3. *How do you open any files today created with that older software?*

   b. What spreadsheet software do you use?

   c. Do you create presentations using software?

   d. Do you use any contact management software?

   e. Do you use any databases? (mention Access, Oracle)

      i. Do any of these databases reside on your computer?

      ii. Do you use any databases with custom (internal) names?

2. Do you use any online databases or services (e.g., salesforce.com)?

   a. If so, do you have a unique account, or do you share it with other people?

   b. Who else in your group/department/company uses this database/service?

c. How long have you been using this service?

d. Who pays for this service?

3. Do you use any other software or systems in your work that I haven't mentioned yet?

4. Do you do your own typing? For everything, or just e-mail messages? If not, who does?

5. Do you keep a formal calendar? Using a program like Outlook? Do you add your own entries? If not, who does?

6. Do you use a Blackberry, Blackjack, Sidekick, Treo, or other smartphone? Do you use a PDA, like a PalmPilot, PocketPC, or Sharp Wizard?

a. How long have done so / Did you ever do so?

b. How do you use your device?

c. What information do you keep on this device?

d. If you have stopped using the device or upgraded it, what happened to the older one?

Preservation of Evidence

1. When and how did you learn about this lawsuit?

2. Did anyone tell you to preserve electronic data that relates to this lawsuit and not erase any of it?

a. When did you get this instruction?

b. Were the instructions written or oral?

c. Did you get any follow-up training or reminders?

d. Since [date of the lawsuit], have you deleted any files from your computer that might have related to this lawsuit?

e. Since [date of the lawsuit], have you deleted any files from your computer at all? How did you check to see whether they were not relevant to this lawsuit?

3. Have you been asked by anyone since [commencement of lawsuit] to delete any files on any computer to which you have access, whether at work or at home or elsewhere?

4. Do you know what it is to "defragment" the hard drive in your computer? If so, have you ever run such a program to defragment it?

5. Do you know what it means to "wipe" a hard drive? If so, have you ever run software that will "wipe" a drive? Where? When? Why?

6. Does your company have a written e-mail policy concerning use of corporate computer equipment and internet access?

   a. Does it include discussion about who owns the e-mail, expectations of privacy, or any other policy relating to e-mail?

   b. How long has this policy been in place?

   c. Do you know if it has ever been amended?

   d. Who is the author of the current policy?

   e. Do you have a copy of the policy?

7. Does your company have a written policy concerning the retention and destruction of paper records?

   a. If so, how long has that policy been in place?

   b. Do you know if it has ever been amended?

   c. Who is the author of the current policy?

   d. Do you have a copy of the policy?

8. Does your company have a written policy concerning the retention and destruction of electronic records (such as files generated by computers, voice mail, e-mail)?

   a. If so, how long has that policy been in place?

   b. Do you know if it has ever been amended?

    c. Who is the author of the current policy?

    d. Do you have a copy of the policy?

9. Does your company have a disaster recovery plan?

Third-party Sources of Information

1. Do you send e-mail from your work account to people outside the company?

    a. parent company or corporate subsidiary?

    b. outside consultants?

    c. government agencies?

    d. investors or other parties to this lawsuit [hereinafter = "outside entity"]?

    e. What are the reasons you are in contact with these individuals or organizations?

2. Do you regularly receive e-mail from people outside the company?

    a. Who are your most common correspondents?

    b. Why do you communicate with them?

    c. What do they do at their companies?

3. Do you receive voice mail from time to time from [a specific outside entity]?

4. What is the most often-used medium of document exchange between [outside entity] and you: e-mail, fax, regular mail, or something else?

5. How frequent are your communications with [outside entity] (i.e. daily, once a week, monthly)? Has there ever been a significant period of time (i.e. more than ___ weeks) when there was no communication between you and [outside entity]? If so, was that, if you know, due to technical problems of any kind, such as computer system failures?

6. Do you have any communications with [outside entity] through use of collaborative software, such as "white boarding" over the Internet with something like Microsoft's NetMeeting, or through use of a Web site where people can meet via the Internet and share ideas and thoughts?

7. Is there a site on the Internet where you and [outside entity] post and share information?

8. Is there a site not on the Internet (such as an intranet or extranet) where you and the [outside entity] post and share information?

9. Does [outside entity] have a Web site? If so, what is its Internet address?

10. In conjunction with this lawsuit, has anyone at [outside entity] asked you to look for records or otherwise supply information, either in paper or electronic form? If so, what documents, when, and for what stated purpose?

11. Do you know the kind of computers the [outside entity] uses?

12. Can you estimate how many computers are there?

13. Is there a computer network at [outside entity]?

14. Does the [outside entity] direct you or otherwise expect you to use compatible software?

15. [If foreign entity] Do you know whether the work product [outside entity] creates is in English or in another language? About how much might be in a foreign language?

16. Do you know how incoming e-mail is routed in the [outside entity]?

17. Does [outside entity] have document management software to log incoming and/or outgoing mail?

18. Does [outside entity] have any formal policies on how incoming mail is logged and routed? Does this policy

come from [outside entity] or from another outside entity?

19. Have you ever been told by anyone in [outside entity] that they did not receive e-mail you had sent them? To your knowledge, has lost e-mail been a problem expressed to you by [outside entity]?

20. Who else besides you receives e-mail from the [outside entity]?

21. Besides e-mail, have you ever exchanged documents in electronic form between your company and the [outside entity]? If so, have you ever done so by attaching documents to e-mail? Any other way?

22. Are faxes routinely sent back and forth between you and [outside entity]?

23. Is there a fax log kept of these incoming and outgoing faxes?

24. Do you have such a fax log kept on a computer? If so, how is that log kept and by what software?

25. In sending or receiving a fax between you and [outside entity], has there ever been a fax sent electronically, i.e. from a computer without use of paper? Is that the typical way faxes are sent? (if appropriate: If not, what if anything explains why sometimes a fax would be sent electronically and why at other times by paper?)

26. Have you received any e-mails from [outside entity] concerning this lawsuit?

27. Have you been told by anyone at [outside entity] to do anything with information in your possession or to which you have access, such as to preserve it, destroy it, or anything else?

28. Have you received from or sent e-mails to anyone in [outside entity] in the last ___ years?

29. Have you deleted from your office or home computer(s) any of that e-mail? If so, what and when?

Storage

1. Does your company use backup tapes?

   a. If you do not know, who would?

   b. If you do use backup tapes, where are they stored? (onsite and offsite)

2. What security measures are in place to protect unauthorized access to tapes or other backup media you may be using?

3. Are backups kept on anything other than tapes?

4. What person or persons have custody of those tapes?

5. Who makes the backups? How long has that person been doing that? Who did the backups before that person?

6. What is the brand name and type of backup tapes, if you areusing them?

7. Are the backup tapes labeled? If so, what information is kept on the labels?

8. Have any backup tapes ever been destroyed, erased or altered, to your knowledge? If so, when, where and why?

9. Do you use any streaming backup solutions to a remote site?

   a. Is the remote site part of your company or a third-party repository?

   b. Where is the remote site located?

   c. How long is backup date kept at the remote site?

   d. How often do you perform a backup to this location?

   e. Who manages this backup function at your company?

10. Have you ever had to restore from backup? What was the outcome? How long did it take?

Records Management

1. Do you have a records management (RM) or Enterprise Content Management (ECM) system?

2. Have you used your records management or ECM system?

3. Who administers your records management or ECM system?

4. Do you have a choice as to what documents you put into the records management system or ECM system? Does everything go into the system?

5. Do you choose how your documents are categorized in the RM or ECM system?

6. Can you check documents in and out of the RM or ECM system?

    a. When you check out a document, is a copy still left in the system?

    b. When you check in a document, does it replace an earlier version already in the system?

7. Do you keep documents in places other than the RM or ECM system? Where?

Other Lawsuits

1. Has your company ever produced electronic data to another party in a lawsuit?

    a. If so, in what matter(s)?

    b. What data was produced?

    c. In what format was the electronic data produced (e.g., TIFF or PDF files, native files, produced on CD or DVD-ROM media or hard drive, in paper)?

2. To what party or parties was that data produced?

3. Was any of the electronic data used at trial or in support of any court filings?

4. If electronic documents were used as evidence in a case, what was the name of that case / those cases? In what court(s) was / were those documents filed?

Retired Hardware

1. What is the usual life span of a computer at your company?

2. Is there a practice of computers used at one echelon of the company (for example, top management) migrating to other employees in the company as newer equipment is purchased?

3. What happens to computers and/or their hard drives when they are retired from service?

4. How many computers from _____ to _____ were retired from service, given away or sold? Who would have records that might answer that question? What would you call such records for the purpose of being able to identify them?

Encryption and Legacy Data

1. Do you understand what "encryption" means?

2. Does anyone at your company ever talk about encrypting electronic information, like e-mail messages, spreadsheets, and other files?

3. Does anyone at your company ever talk about using "password protection" to electronic information, like e-mail messages, spreadsheets, and other files?

4. Do you use password protection or encryption for any work product you create using a computer? Do you know whether your colleagues and co-workers use password protection or encryption?

    a. Is this a decision you made on your own, at someone's direction, or as a matter of organization policy?

    b. Is there a written policy regarding use of encryption or password protection?

5. If you use encryption software

a. How long have you been using encryption software?

b. Have you always used the same software?

c. What version of the software are you using?

d. What level of encryption are you using?

e. If not you, who at your organization would know the answer to these questions?

6. How do you decrypt files that you receive as part of your work?

a. Is there a list of common passwords used at your organization?

b. How do you work with encrypted files from former employees or colleagues?

7. Do you maintain older backup tapes, archive tapes, hard drives, or otherwise, for which you no longer actively use the software that created the files on the storage media? [This question is meant to elicit information about "legacy data," electronic data on such old software programs as WordStar, VisiCalc or WANG that cannot easily be read by modern software and equipment]

a. Do you keep a copy of the software used to create these older archives? Have you ever had to use it in the past __ years?

b. Who in your company still knows how to access data on these old tapes and storage media?

c. Do you use a consultant or outside company to help you retrieve information from these old tapes and storage media? If so, who?

APPENDIX G

Data Collection Forms

Receipt of Media Form

PREPARED AT THE REQUEST OF COUNSEL – PRIVILEGED AND CONFIDENTIAL

RECEIVED FROM:

Name ———————————— Title ————————————

Address ————————————————————————————

City ———————————— State ————— Zip —————

Phone (w) ———————————— Ext ————————————

Phone (h) ———————————— Ext ————————————

Cell ———————————— Pager ————— PIN —————

E-mail ————————————————————————————

MEDIA TYPE	SERIAL NUMBER	NOTES

RELEASED TO:

Name ———————————— Title ————————————

Signature ———————————————— Date —————

Phone (w) ———————————— Ext ————————————

Phone (h) ———————————— Ext ————————————

E-mail ————————————————————————————

Desktop Collection Information Form

PREPARED AT THE REQUEST OF COUNSEL – PRIVILEGED AND CONFIDENTIAL

The information below will assist in describing the chain of custody for the data which is collected.

COMPUTER USER: _____

Name _____

E-mail _____

Address _____

City _____ State _____ Zip _____

Phone (w) _____ Ext _____

Phone (h) _____ Ext _____

Cell _____ Pager _____ Pin _____

Title _____ ISID _____

BROUGHT TO YOU? Y/N IF YES, BY WHOM? _____

Name _____

Phone (w) _____ Ext _____

Phone (h) _____ Ext _____

IF NOT BROUGHT TO YOU:

Building _____ Floor _____ Office/Cube/Mailstop _____

Was this the only computer in this person's area? Y/N _____

Location of computer (ex. On desk, under desk, in leather bag) _____

MACHINE/DRIVE IDENTIFIERS:

Type (Laptop, desktop, notebook, server) _____

Manufacturer _____

Model Serial Number _____

Asset/inventory tag _____

NUMBER OF PERIPHERALS ATTACHED TO THE COMPUTER WITH THE COMPUTER OF INTEREST (WRITE 0 IF NONE) ALSO, REMOVABLE MEDIA IN AREA:

Hard drives _____ CD ROM Read Only _____

CD Rom Read/Write _____ Fax/modem _____

3.5 floppy _____ Printer ports _____

Zip/Jaz drive _____ USB ports _____

Docking station _____ Network connection _____

Floppies _____ Tapes _____

CD Roms _____ Zip, Jaz _____

Other not listed _____

NOTES: _____

Bios date/time _____ Actual date/time _____

Name of Ghost image _____

Copied to network drive _____

TYPE OF DATA	NAME	DATE COLLECTED	COLLECTED BY
Home directory			
User computer			
E-mail			
Share 1			
Share 2			

GATHERER'S INFORMATION AND SIGNATURE:

Signature _____

Name _____

Gathered at the request of _____

Case identifier _____

© Copyright 2000-2007, Fios, Inc.

Server Information Form

PREPARED AT THE REQUEST OF COUNSEL-PRIVILEGED AND CONFIDENTIAL

LOCATION: _____ Server _____

ON SITE CONTACT: _____

Name _____ Title _____

Address _____

City _____ State _____ Zip _____

Phone (w) _____ Ext _____

Phone (h) _____ Ext _____

Cell _____ Pager _____ Pin _____

E-mail (w) _____

E-mail (h) _____

PHYSICAL LOCATION:

Secure location? Y/N ____ If yes, type of access (e.g. Keycard, code) _____

Phone (in room) _____ Ext _____

Building _____ Floor _____ Room _____

Location of computer (e.g. Rack #, Shelf) _____

HARDWARE:

Machine name _____

Manufacturer _____

Domain name _____

Model _____ Serial #

Asset tag # _____

Tape drive manufacturer _____

Model # _____ Serial #

Tape media size _____

TIME:

Bios date/time _____

Actual date/time _____

Time zone _____

Daylight savings selected? _____

SOFTWARE:

Operating system version and service pack _____

Exchange version and service pack _____

Site name _____

Organization name _____

Exmerge version _____

Backup software/version _____

Open file agent? _____

GATHERER'S INFORMATION AND SIGNATURE:

Name _____ Title _____

Signature _____

Company _____

Phone (w) _____ Ext _____

Phone (h) _____ Ext _____

E-mail (w) _____

E-mail (h) _____

Key Personnel List

PREPARED AT THE REQUEST OF COUNSEL-PRIVILEGED AND CONFIDENTIAL

LOCATION: _____

ROLE	NAME/DEPARTMENT	PHONE/E-MAIL
Top Manager		
Top IT Manager		
E-mail		
Network		
Desktop		
Security		
Help Desk		
Telecom		
Human Resources		

© *Copyright 2000-2008, Fios, Inc.*

About the Author

Mary Mack, Esq.
Corporate Technology Counsel
Fios, Inc.

Mary Mack brings legal and technical professionals from law firms, enterprises and service providers together in a focused collaboration to generate and execute a successful, cost-effective course of compliance with electronic discovery requests. As Corporate Technology Counsel for Fios, she has more than 25 years experience delivering enterprise-wide electronic discovery, managed services and software projects with legal and IT departments in publicly held companies. Mary is a hands-on strategic advisor to counsel for some of the most mission critical products liability class actions, government investigations and intellectual property disputes. Clients include the largest law firms, pharmaceutical companies and insurance companies in the world.

A member of the Illinois Bar, ACC and the ABA's Section on Litigation, Mary received her J.D. from Northwestern University School of Law (1982) and a B.A. from LeMoyne College in Syracuse, NY. She holds certifications in Computer Forensics and Computer Telephony.

Mary is one of the leading speakers and authors on electronic discovery issues, technology and the law. She hosts the blog, "Sound Evidence," featured on DiscoveryResources.org and is regularly featured as an expert in the leading magazines and newspapers, such as The New York Times, InsideCounsel Magazine, Law.com, Chicago Lawyer, Compliance Week and Metropolitan Corporate Counsel Magazine. Her new book, "e-Discovery for Corporate Counsel," co-authored with Carol Basri, is being published by West in the second half of 2008.

LaVergne, TN USA
14 February 2010
173053LV00001B/11/P